MW01057756

CAUGHT IN THE NET

ACKNOWLEDGEMENTS

To former members of my basketball coaching staff, including Bobby Knight, Darrell Hedric, Charlie Harrison, Bill Clendinen, Mike Steele and Tommy Barrise. Without their efforts my job would have been impossible.

To my former NBA boss, Jack Ramsay, for his cooperation and understanding.

Above all to my former players at Clemson University. I know the personal hell I lived through in my five seasons at that school and I often wonder how those years affected them as human beings.

A special thank you, in particular, to Wayne "Tree" Rollins and Colon Abraham, whose willingness to come forth in support of this book was greatly appreciated.

To our friends Charlie Shad, Tom Cornelison of the Jacksonville Journal, Milt Northrup of the Buffalo Evening News, Clemson sports information director Bob Bradley and former Jacksonville sports information director Bill Goldring, now SID at Indiana State.

A special thank you to Mrs. James Grier.

To Vera, who knows why, and to Judy Ferro for her assistance in proofreading and typing the manuscript.

And deepest thanks and love to our parents, Ed and Glenna Locke and Robert and the late Elinore Ibach.

CAUGHT IN THE NET

by
Tates Locke
Bob Ibach

Leisure Press
P.O. Box
West Point, NY 10996

A publication of Leisure Press
P.O. Box 3, West Point, N.Y. 10996
Copyright © 1982 Leisure Press
All rights reserved. Printed in the U.S.A.

ISBN 0-88011-044-9
Library of Congress Number: 81-36382

Cover design: Diana J. Goodin
Back Cover Photo: *Florida Times-Union*
(© Florida Publishing Company)
Illustrations: Suzanne K. M. Marcy

PHOTO CREDITS

Miami University (Ohio) Audio Visual Service: 48, 51.
U.S. Army Photograph: 49, 50.
Clemson University Sports Information Office: 52 (top), 53, 54 (all),
    55, 106 (all), 107, 108, 110 (all), 111 (top and lower left), 112, 113.
Wilton E. Hall: 52 (bottom).
James T. Hammond (*News-Piedmont*): 105.
Terry Dickson: 109.
Kansas City Kings: 111 (lower right).
Bill Mount: 62.
Robert L. Smith (*Buffalo Evening News*): 160 (top).
Ronald J. Lolleran (*Buffalo Evening News*): 160 (bottom).
Dennis C. Enser: 161.
Florida Times Union: 162, 163 (both), Outside Back Cover.

CONTENTS

CAUGHT IN THE NET

1
APRIL FOOL

I was having a hard time getting to sleep. Nothing too unusual about that. There are a lot of other head college basketball coaches in this country who don't sleep all that well in the springtime.

To be quite blunt about it, there aren't many houses in this country that are clean these days.

March and April. Those months are the harvest season for a basketball coach, when every blue-chip high school prospect in the fold brings you a step closer to sold-out arenas, television revenue, national attention and, of course, personal job security. Let's not forget that last one. I mean, the public may judge you by how well your team performs on the court between November and April but there's not a coach out there today who is foolish enough to believe he can keep his job by simply being a good tactician.

There's more to it than that. The bottom line is that a coach has to win some of the "games" held *off* the court in the spring. Of course, we're talking about recruiting. It's a flesh market, really. The hardest part is not finding the prospect—we all know where the good ones are located. No, the difficult part is getting these kids to sign that document called a grant-in-aid. It's one big rodeo and you've got to go out and get some horses. Some real studs. And that's what April and March are all about—corraling those horses in your barn.

In that respect, the spring of 1981 was going along quite well for me and my staff at Jacksonville University. We had gone after and signed a couple of highly touted prospects, a 6-4 guard named Calvin Duncan from Virginia and a 6-10 center, Dave Reickenicker of Florida. We lost a good kid, too.

We had followed 7-1 center Warren Martin all across the state of Virginia for a couple months but wound up losing him to North Carolina and their coach Dean Smith. I remember the day well; it was the same day an attempt was made to assassinate President Reagan. It was a pretty bad day all around.

We had gone 8-19 in 1980-81 after seasons of 19-11 and 20-9 my first two years at the Sun Belt Conference school. Eight and nineteen. The thought of it chewed at my insides all spring. It was like someone was playing ping pong inside my stomach. We were coming off the worst season ever, in terms of wins and losses, of any team I had coached since my Clemson University squad went 9-17 in 1971.

Come to think of it, 1980-81 had been my worst season *ever* in 14 years of coaching college basketball, even though my JU players hustled and never quit trying. In fact, quite often we had far better statistics than some of the teams which defeated us, but that doesn't really mean much. I'm not one for believing in statistics.

In a perverse way, 1980-81 hadn't been all that bad. Oh, don't misunderstand, I *hate* to lose, just hate it, but this time around I was able to deal with the defeats. Maybe it was because we were playing to our expectations. We simply didn't have that much talent.

After we lost in the opening round of the Sun Belt post-season tournament in late February, I vowed there would be no repeat of 1980-81. "Never Again" became my personal battle cry. I wasn't trying to con myself, either. I believed it.

I kept searching for the light at the end of the tunnel. I told myself that worse things had happened to me in my career than going 8-19. Dammit, at least it was an HONEST 8-19. There had been times in the past when I couldn't have looked a guy square in the eye and said the same about some of my other ballclubs, teams that had won as many as 17 games. Yes, I had won a lot of games...but I had also cheated on occasion to win.

Hey, I'm not particularly proud of the way I conducted myself during five seasons at Clemson, from 1970 to 1975. It's a dark cloud that still hangs over me. I became known as an outlaw coach. I still carry that reputation even today. It's almost as if I've got a scarlet letter hanging around my neck. In a way I'm no better off than Hester Prynne. I did, and I do, have a mark against me.

I try not to dwell on it but it hurts me when I pick up an article and I see references to those times at Clemson. It gives me a low that day, especially if I feel that an administrator may have made that remark.

The sad part about this business is that once you're marked, it matters not how you got marked, or how badly you got marked. The administrators look down their noses at you, not even concerned that they might be standing knee-deep in it themselves. But that's another story which I'll get to later.

At Jacksonville, it had been different. It had to be. The marriage to JU was a good one for both myself and the school. It was the outlaw coach coming in to take over the outlaw school. You see, we needed each other. We could use each other for mutual benefit.

Both of us were walking a tightrope. Personally, I had done quite well in my first two jobs. At Army, in 1964 and 1965, I coached teams which won 19 and 21 games. Both seasons we finished third in the National Invitation Tournament. Then in 1966 I went to Miami of Ohio, winning 56 games in four seasons. My 1969 team was runnerup in the NCAA Regional and we went to the NIT. I was named Mid-American Conference "Coach of the Year".

Then came Clemson. I got caught up in the geographical beauty of a campus in a small South Carolina town and the emotion of coaching in the prestigious Atlantic Coast Conference. I really felt when I took the job at Clemson that *coaching* was still the most important overall factor in winning or losing. I thought you could make chicken salad out of chicken crap.

We went 9-17 that first season in 1970-71. We were the doormat of the league and soon I got pretty tired of losing, getting my brains beat out in the ACC. That's when I decided that players make better chicken salad. It was a bad decision. I should have walked away from the situation but I didn't.

The situation was very similar at Jacksonville, only the Dolphins were experiencing a "high" when I was at my lowest at Clemson. In 1970, JU was led to the NCAA championship finals against UCLA by center Artis Gilmore, now playing professionally in the NBA with the Chicago Bulls. Soon after, JU's basketball fortunes declined. By 1978, when the school hired me as its head coach, basketball was near its death.

Not only wasn't the school winning games, but the image of JU basketball *off* the court was ugly. When I arrived, several players were alleged to be heavily involved in drugs and another was even arrested for shooting a fellow teammate. It wasn't a pretty scene.

I remember one local writer telling me about the school's problems and he remarked that the Dolphins were the only team which cut down the net after a victory with switchblades. I heard that, even if it was said in jest, and I knew I had my work cut out. I was going to be the heavy...the gunslinger. The fellow who restored law and order. Well, if JU wanted a tough guy, they found one.

Let me put it this way: I don't rip into my ballplayers just for the sake of cutting open an asshole. There's a method to my madness, if you will. I want disciplined young men playing ball for me, guys who will reach down inside their gut and give a little more of themselves. I thoroughly enjoy coaching young men on a basketball court. Young men, not boys. Sure I rip into them hard sometimes but I've loved every one of my players.

All I've ever tried to do with any of them is make them better people, not just better basketball players. Send them out into the world with a better chance to succeed. Look, you've got to be tough or that real world out there will consume you. You've got to be ready for anything.

Well, *almost* anything. After all, nobody told me I'd be getting fired from my job at Jacksonville on April Fool's Day without further pay.

There are some days in your life that you never forget. April 1, 1981 will be one of them for me. It was shortly after six that evening when I opened the front door to my house. I was an emotional mess, almost beside myself with hurt and anger.

My eyes caught Nancy and the kids as I walked into the living room. I could tell they already knew.

Those bastards, I thought to myself. Those rotten bastards. The damn JU administration hadn't even given me time to drive from the campus to my house to tell my wife and kids. No, Nancy and my children had to hear it on the evening news. A lot of class, huh?

Like I said, I was in pieces when I got home. Just in pieces. I kept telling myself, over and over, that I hadn't done anything wrong. I hadn't cheated, I hadn't lied and I hadn't stolen. I must have said those words over and over and over.

It was unbelievable. We had had only one bad year at JU. Just one. Now, all of a sudden they tell me they don't like my personality. All of a sudden I was outspoken. Essentially, that is what it all came down to—that I was outspoken. That was my first impression at the time and later I discovered it had been the right one. Members of the JU Board of Trustees, mainly a few people from a local food chain who were JU Booster Club members, some guys who I had little or no use for, banded together. That's what they did. They saw an opening and took advantage of it.

Looking back at the April 1 meeting in the administration building, I figured JU president Dr. Frances Kinne was calling me in to give me some good news about my summer basketball camp. I had wanted to hold the camp on campus but the school had hiked the price up some 300 percent, making it impossible for me to make financial ends meet. But President Kinne had talked to me only a few days before and her exact words were, "I think we can come up with a way that we can get this thing resolved." So I was led to believe that our meeting, set for 5 p.m. April 1, was going to be about my camp.

Another possibility for discussion at the meeting, I thought, was the selection of a new athletic director. I had offered some input into this area already, not in terms of who was going to be the new AD, but rather on what basis we should select the individual. So those were my assumptions for the meeting—my camp and discussion of a new athletic director.

When I arrived at Dr. Kinne's fourth floor office it was a couple minutes after five. The number one JU basketball booster, Doug Milne, was already there. He had been a friend of the school's basketball program for a long time. He was a big financial contributor and a member of the Board of Trustees. Doug had helped pull JU's athletic program out of the doldrums many times.

So Milne was there. That made sense. And Dr. Kinne was there. Naturally, that made sense. But there was someone in the room who had no real reason to be in attendance.

I thought to myself, 'Why was Robert Shircliff there?'

Shircliff was the president of the Board of Trustees but he had about as much interest in basketball as...well, he had *no* interest at all in the sport. I guess when I saw Shircliff was when I realized the meeting might have been called for another reason. Perhaps they were going to scold me for something I had said in the newspapers.

Sometimes I know what I say hits home kind of hard. I don't pull punches when it comes to mixing words. I had been vocal about the horrible conditions at Swisher Gym, where some of my players spent their spare time trapping rats. The locker room there was a real hole. I had gotten on JU fans sometimes, too. I remember once calling them "rats deserting a sinking ship" after they left the arena early in a game which we were losing. And yes, sometimes I came down heavy on some of my players. I was only trying to motivate them.

I never said one of my players was a bad person. I never said one of them had bad character. It's my right as a coach to criticize my players but I wouldn't question the meat they put out on the counter in a grocery store or a doctor's prognosis.

I've always felt the people that challenge you on something like that usually have social problems at home with their own kids. Everyone who came down on me had some ugly things going on in their own homes.

I always told my players to listen to what I say, not *how* I said it. And no matter what I said I still loved them. I remember the last game I coached at JU, against South Florida in the tournament. Mo Roulhac had two free throws coming at the end of the game and I told him in the huddle, "Whether you make them or miss them, I still love you." People don't know that. They believe everything they read or hear.

Like I said, maybe Shircliff was going to get on me for something I had said. That's the only thing I could think of.

When I entered the room, Shircliff was very friendly to me. In fact he started talking about the NCAA championships which had been played in Philadelphia two days earlier. Shircliff knew that Indiana's coach, Bobby Knight, was probably my best friend. He's probably the best friend I have, period. He was my assistant coach at West Point. Bobby and I go back a long way. We've been through some wars together.

Anyway, Shircliff and I started talking about how Bobby's team had defeated North Carolina. Indiana had actually a rather easy time beating Dean Smith's team for the national championship. We were talking basketball when, all of a sudden, everybody sat down in their chairs and Shircliff got real quiet.

I looked around the room and it struck me as somewhat peculiar as to the way the chairs had been neatly arranged. How precisely everyone had gone to their respective positions, as if by design. Milne sat on one side of me and Dr. Kinne sat on the other. Shircliff took the seat directly in front of me.

Shircliff did all the talking.

"Now we gotta get to the unpleasant stuff," Shircliff began. He was looking down at one of those yellow legal pads. He was fidgeting.

"We're asking you to resign."

I swallowed hard. He was asking me to do what? I was looking straight at Shircliff. I couldn't believe what he had said. Finally, after about 15 seconds, I spoke up.

"Wait a minute. No...no...no. Wait a minute. This is a joke, right?"

"No, this isn't a joke," Shircliff shot back.

"Then if it isn't, why in the hell am I resigning?"

Then Shircliff looked back down at that yellow pad and began reading off a bunch of reasons. First, he said, I was outspoken about university facilities. Secondly, he said, I was negligent in administering to university automobiles. You see, my assistant coach, Tommy Barrise, had several accidents. I mean I don't think Tommy ever turned a car back in that *hadn't* been involved in some kind of scrape. He had a perfect record. But it was no big deal. The car dealers were still giving the school new cars for us to use.

The third reason, according to the school, was that I had been delinquent in my payments from my summer basketball camp in 1980. But what they *forgot* to say was that I had a contract and a letter of agreement with the JU business manager which gave me until June of 1981 to pay back that money. By my calendar, it still wasn't June. I had all intentions of meeting that obligation.

There were other charges, too. They said I had purchased tee-shirts for my own selfish reasons. Well, I did buy 3,000 tee-shirts but that was something I did through the JU Boosters Club. What the hell was I going to do with 3,000 tee-shirts for myself? The shirts had nothing to do with my basketball camp. I had bought them for the Boosters Club because they had asked me to buy them. I had gotten a helluva deal on the shirts and they wanted to use them for promotions.

Another problem concerned my failure to check with the administration before offering Harley "Skeeter" Swift a position as an assistant coach on my staff in the spring of 1981. Actually, I wasn't sure both of my assistants would be staying and it was in anticipation of having to make a change that

I discussed such an opening with Swift.

The charge that I had brought Swift and his family to JU at the expense of the University was also erroneous. His only paid visit to campus came in the fall of 1980, when he was brought to school to conduct a coaching clinic.

Those were the reasons, or so they said. I remember turning to Shircliff and saying, "You mean that's it?" and his reply being, "It's just your overall attitude."

Then he started talking about "this thing". I knew what Shircliff was referring to. "This thing" was my being interviewed for the head coaching position at Mississippi State.

Let me explain the Mississippi State "thing". Let me put the facts on the table. To begin with, I never went after the job. Mississippi State athletic director Carl Maddox was the one who invited me to their campus. Actually, it began when Hootie Ingram, now AD at Florida State, recommended me to Mississippi State. Hootie had been the head football coach at Clemson when I was coaching basketball at that school. Well, Hootie got in touch with Maddox, who in turn, called our acting athletic director, Judson Harris, to get his permission. I believe the contact with Harris was made on either March 16 or 17. That's when Mississippi State got permission to talk with me. They got permission from Harris!

But I don't think Harris ever relayed the conversation to President Kinne or anyone else. At the time, Dr. Kinne was going through some hard times personally. Her husband had cancer and she was going back and forth to the Mayo Clinic in Rochester, Minnesota. During her absence, Bob Augspurger, the school vice president and business manager, basically took over running the university. What I didn't realize was this guy had it in for me. I really don't know why.

Augspurger had made numerous comments which had gotten back to me. Those comments led me to believe that he thought I was just too big for my britches. Comments like, "Why was sports everything?" Or "Who was I?" He made comments like that, I was told, regularly. I never heard about them until they got back to me after I was dismissed.

About a week before the meeting in Dr. Kinne's office I flew to Starkville, Mississippi to meet with Maddox. I was only going as a favor to Hootie. He said the situation at Mississippi State was very similar to the one I had encountered at Clemson, that Maddox would be appreciative of anything I could offer in helping them choose the candidate. I told Hootie I was content with my position at JU, but I figured I owed him a favor and I went to Starkville on March 25. I asked Shircliff how they could hold something like that against me.

"We just don't think you have any loyalties," Shircliff responded.

"No loyalties. Does the school have any loyalties to me?" I asked.

13

"What about the promises you made to me when you hired me about cleaning up the facilities around here?"

I went through all of that with him, how some of my players weren't given a decent place to live. I spent some of my own money to get them into better apartments. I was picking up the difference. Those kids weren't getting the full amount of aid monies they should have been receiving. Almost every kid on the squad was on BEOG. That stands for Basic Economic Opportunity Grant. The school got anywhere from one-third to one-half of that grant back...and was not putting any of it toward the kids' housing. That really pissed me off.

In reality, if a scholarship was worth $5,000 and JU was getting $2,000 from the government, the entire $5,000 was not being put into that scholarship for the player.

After we had hashed at this for a few minutes, I finally turned to President Kinne and asked, "Are you in accord with all of these charges?"

"This has been a vote of the Board of Trustees," she replied.

Later I would find out that Dr. Kinne fought for me. So did Milne. Still, I was out of a job.

Locke has been fired, aide says

Jacksonville University officials, including President Frances Kinne, met today to officially fire basketball coach Tates Locke, a member of Locke's staff said.

Although school officials would not confirm the firing was official, a Locke aide said, "It's official. Coach has been fired. No matter what else you have heard, coach has been fired."

Still another school official said, "We are now consulting with legal counsel and are not ready to announce anything at this time. We don't want to go off half-cocked. We would rather wait until everything is official."

Assistant Coach Tom Barisse conducted a team meeting at the school today and informed the Dolphin players that Locke was being fired.

Earlier in the day prior to the early afternoon conference, Locke made it clear he had no intention of resigning.

"I have not resigned and have no intention of resigning," Locke said. "I have four years left on my contract and it now becomes a legal matter."

Locke did confirm, however, that he walked out of a meeting yesterday with Dr. Kinne, JU Board of Trustees chairman Robert Shircliff and Doug Milne, a prominent JU booster and former head of the board of trustees.

"That may have been defined as a resignation by the people in the room, but not by me," Locke said. "True, I was asked to resign several times but never did I say I was resigning."

TATES LOCKE

Locke added, "I was called into the meeting without any previous warning that anybody was unhappy with the way I was running the basketball program at JU. He (Shircliff) started talking in generalities about how displeased they were with the way I handled my administrative duties and some of the things I had been quoted on publicly critizing the facilities at the school. But no mention was made about how I coached basketball.

"At one point, he (Shircliff) said, 'I guess you could say we're asking you to resign.' I gave no answer and the conversation reached the point to where I would either say something I might regret later or cry.

"When it reached the breaking point, I got up and said, 'I'm going home to talk to my family.'"

Locke went on to say, "I walked out of the building in the rain and I was dumbfounded that before I had time to get home my family had heard I had resigned. It's amazing how quickly it reached the media . . . even before I got home."

Meanwhile at JU today, Mary Anne Rogers, director of public relations at the school, said, "Our position is that he has resigned and we're in the process of appointing a search committee for a new coach. We hope to announce the members of that committee later today."

15

JU-Locke divorce will be best for both parties

The divorce of basketball Coach Tates Locke and Jacksonville University did not have to happen now and it did not have to be the sloppy affair that it turned out to be.

But the marriage could not last. Eventually, there had to be a parting of the ways.

Each turned to the other in time of need and each used the other for mutual benefit but, in the future, Locke will be better off without JU and JU will be better off without Locke.

At first, the alliance was built out of need. Locke had been all but black-balled from his profession for recruiting violations at Clemson and JU provided a second chance. Because he had been burned once, Locke knew rival coaches would keep an eye on his program and that his operation had to be run within the NCAA rules.

And JU needed a bath. Its outlaw image was well deserved. One writer once penned that the Dolphins were the only team that cut down the net after a win with switchblades. A tough guy was needed.

Locke was perfect for the part. He was the gunslinger from the grade B movie who cleaned up the town only to find he was out of place when peace and progress were restored. To be more specific, JU is a young, small and private school which is not going to provide its coach with a Notre Dame-sized budget.

Locke wanted good things for his program and players — an on-campus gym, a weight room, an intercollegiate athletic department completely separate from the physical education department, a renovated practice facility.

Dolphin boosters and school administrators had nothing against Locke's dreams, but they were more realistic than he was. Said one prominent backer after yesterday's bloodletting, "He knew what the facilities were like when he came here."

From an economic standpoint, Locke's absolute refusal to live within a budget was probably the greatest factor leading to the loss of his job. When he expressed dissatisfaction with the arrangement for his summer basketball camp, nobody in high places at JU sympathized. Locke's side of the story is that the school doubled the price of room and board. The school's unannounced side of the story is that Locke still owes $11,000 from last year's camp.

From an image standpoint, Locke went full circle from being an asset to a liability. His criticizing of officials and JU players in terms just this side of libel sounded colorful when he was winning, but came across as a string of alibis when he was losing. For an institution which proudly believes it is making strong academic strides, Locke's choice of words was a frequent embarrassment.

Tom Cornelison
Journal Sports Writer

The final two blows were Locke's delay in signing a five-year contract extended to him in the midst of the worst losing streak in Dolphin history, and his trip to Mississippi State for a job interview last week.

It took class and guts for JU president Dr. Frances Kinne to offer the contract, and Locke should be faulted for not signing. However, he should not be faulted for listening to what another school had to offer.

Yesterday, when it was announced State had hired former Southern California Coach Bob Boyd, Locke talked optimistically of next season at JU. That was before a 4:30 meeting with Kinne, long-time JU booster Doug Milne and JU Board Of Trustees chairman Robert Shircliff. Locke angrily left the meeting, and the school announced he resigned.

But Locke told his staff and team that he did not resign. He prides himself on never re-

signing from anything in his life. This is true. What happened yesterday amounted to a firing, even if the words "You're fired" were never used until today.

Give Locke credit for cleaning up the image of the JU athlete. If the NCAA and NIT bids plus the 39 wins of his first two seasons at the school were the result of having James Ray in the lineup, it must also be pointed out that a far more talented Dolphin team which included Ray went 14-14 the year before Locke arrived. But Locke also deserves blame for a poor record of recruiting at JU, which directly resulted in last year's 8-19 season.

What happens next? A search committee will be formed in the next 48 hours to find a successor. The school will also be in touch with the two prospects who have signed to play for the Dolphins next year — 6-4 guard Calvin Duncan and 6-10 center Dave Reickenicker. Duncan, the more highly-regarded of the two, indicated he still intends to play for JU.

There is talk from the best returning player on the roster — Mike Hackett — that he will transfer, but he will be better off waiting to see who the new coach is and what he has to say. Several players are planning to approach Dr. Kinne on behalf of Locke, but this will do no good. He's gone. The school will pay him through Sept. 1, provided he does not accept

another job before then. At the moment, Locke has no plans.

As for a successor, the most logical choice is a sharp, young assistant coach from a major program who is looking for a chance to move up. There is no George Steinbrenner to help hire a Lee Rose here. If the young assistant has Jacksonville ties, it will help.

A name? Just for the sake of discussion, how about 29-year-old George Scholz, a JU graduate who has been an assistant at Iowa and South Alabama and is currently at Missouri. In keeping with the academic pride the institution is trying to build, Scholz has co-authored a book: *Basketball: Building The Complete Program.*

Other names will surface. What the next JU coach must realize is that the school wants to be competitive on a national level, but also wants the most mileage out of its resources. The Dolphins won't be an annual power. The goal will have to be to build toward peak years, and then rebuild again.

Quick injections of strength to the program by signing academically risky players won't be tolerated as it was in the days before Locke. But neither will the schemes and dreams which has led to the days after Locke.

2
ALONE AGAIN . . . NATURALLY

There were a lot of rumors circulating around Jacksonville after my dismissal. I'm sure some people around the country, remembering what happened to me at Clemson in 1975, felt I must have got my hands caught in the cookie jar again.

I don't worry about what others think because I never cheated at Jacksonville. Before I came to JU I knew that if I ever got a chance to coach at the college level again that people would be watching me closely day and night. And I knew that if I ever got caught cheating again I'd never get another chance to coach.

In other words, JU was going to be my last shot.

Looking back, I don't feel any shame about what happened at Jacksonville. I mean, I know what I am and I know there are a helluva lot of people out there who can't stand up with their head held high. I don't feel any guilt or shame. I did when I got fired at Clemson.

I'm not going to second guess myself for what occurred at JU. I was totally above board. I never did anything dishonest. I guess the only thing I would have done differently was to cover my back. I let some people do some things to me that I shouldn't have. But basically, I would not have done anything any differently if I had it to do over again.

That includes my relationship with Patti Anonsen, a 24-year-old blonde and a former student at JU who is now the athletic director at Bartram School in Jacksonville. I had been seeing Patti for about two years. It was no big secret because the administration knew that Nancy and I had separated. In fact, we had signed a separation agreement dated June 26, 1979. It stated in part:

"It shall be lawful for each of the parties at all times hereafter to live and continue to live separate and apart from each other and to reside from time to time at such place or places and with such person or persons, as either of them may see fit."

That day at our meeting, Shircliff never mentioned Patti but I sensed it was on his mind. So I brought her name up myself.

"If one of the things that's bothering you is the relationship I've had with Patti..."

Everyone got quiet. Then I continued.

"Look, if a person is doing a pretty decent job in one area (coaching) and there are other areas in which he is not doing a good job, in your estimation wouldn't you take that person aside and explain it to him? Wouldn't you get him to change his ways?

"Christ, you people have never communicated to me about this subject in all my time here. Wouldn't it have been easier for you to stand me up in front of the guillotine and let the Board of Trustees rake me over the fire? Try to correct it?"

No one answered my questions.

Though they never told me to my face, it came out later that the administration said it had told me of their disapproval of me dating a JU coed. That's a lie. They never did. First of all, Patti was not a coed. She had graduated from JU. But that is just a technicality. Look, if they had ever told me to quit seeing her, that it was causing some big problem, I would have cut it out. But when I wanted to bring some of this up at the meeting that day, Shircliff got real huffy. All he could say was, "We just want your resignation."

They should have known better. I would never resign. I've never walked away from or quit a job in my life.

Why did they want my resignation? Obviously, so they could legally terminate the remaining four years of my contract. I had signed a renewal September 1, 1980 for five more seasons at an annual salary of $34,500. I was the second lowest paid coach in the Sun Belt Conference.

On February 5, 1981, I received a letter from President Kinne (page 19).

I never signed the reappointment contract. First of all, I had already signed a five-year agreement in September. I had a valid contract for four more seasons. The way I read the "new" contract, as stated in the reappointment letter from Dr. Kinne, is that the agreement would be valid for only *one* year beyond September 1, 1981. In essence, by signing the "new" contract, I was *losing* three guaranteed years of my original five-year agreement.

Along with all of this we were in the middle of the basketball season and I was doing a lot of recruiting. Those were my top priorities, *not* signing a reappointment contract. But unless the university has forgotten, I didn't ig-

OFFICE OF THE PRESIDENT

JACKSONVILLE UNIVERSITY

February 5, 1981

JACKSONVILLE FLORIDA 32211

904 / 744-3950

Mr. Taylor O. Locke
Head Basketball Coach
Jacksonville University

Dear Mr. Locke:

It is a pleasure to inform you of your reappointment for the
contract year beginning September 1, 1981, with an increased
salary of $37,400.

During this year of transition and challenge, it has been
particularly helpful to have your interest, dedication,
service and devotion. Certainly Jacksonville University
is the sum total of the wonderful people who work for this
institution!

Please indicate your acceptance of reappointment by signing
the enclosed copy and returning it to me in an envelope
marked "Confidential" by February 15, 1981.

May 1981 be a happy, creative, productive year for all of
us.

Sincerely,

Frances Bartlett Kinne
President

FBK:mr

nore Dr. Kinne's gesture. In fact, I was quoted by several local writers concerning my deep appreciation for her support and "class" of the university for offering me a contract with a salary increase. I hardly ignored acknowledgement of that new contract as the school later claimed.

Looking back, it turned out to be just one more reason the board used to justify their decision to fire me. Oh yes, they did *fire* me. On April 1 the school issued a four paragraph press release titled: Coach Locke Resigns as JU Basketball Coach. On April 2, another release was issued to the media. This one was headlined: Tates Locke Terminated at JU.

What a difference a day makes, huh?

For me, the next few weeks were a blur. It was like one of those times when you know something bad has happened to you but you can't actually *believe* it really happened. My immediate reaction? Well, I thought the end of the world had come.

For awhile I sat back and brooded. I did some heavy drinking, though not as much as I had done after Clemson fired me six years earlier. But I did start hitting the bottle and drinking beer. I really broke down, especially this one afternoon at our beach house, the place where I had often gone to think out a deep problem, or gone to plot some mid-season basketball strategy. It was my little hideaway, a lovely place, only a couple blocks from the ocean. It was real peaceful. I loved that house and took a lot of pride in remodeling it. When I purchased it, the place was in terrible shape.

On this particular day in April, I had gone there to sort out my life. It was about a week or so after my dismissal. My 15-year-old son, John, had come along to keep me company. A good thing, because not long after we had arrived I broke down totally. I just went to pieces. John had to get Charlie Shad, a neighbor a few houses away who later handled my court suit against Jacksonville University. Charlie is not only a super attorney, but a good friend. He was there when I needed him that day.

Charlie and I went for a long walk along the beach. I remember him saying to me, "Tates, we'll go after 'em. I promise you we will." I told Charlie I didn't have a helluva lot of money to offer him for legal fees but he told me it didn't matter. Charlie was ticked off at the school himself.

Slowly I began to get myself back together mentally. My first rational thoughts were to make sure I got my staff other jobs. Tommy Barrise and Mike Steele, my two young assistant coaches, had contracts at JU through the summer. Still, I knew the new head coach would be bringing in his own people so I had to find them jobs. I also had to try and help my sports information director, Bill Goldring. It was obvious Bill wasn't going to be around JU much longer, either.

They were all loyal fellows and I was concerned they would find themselves out on the street because of me. Tommy took the situation very hard. Shortly after the April 1 meeting with the school officials, I had gone back to my office before driving home. I wanted to tell my staff before they heard about it on television. I'll never forget Tommy's reaction. He was so mad he bolted out of my office and ran toward the administration building. He was going after those people—physically. It took two rent-a-cops to get him out of that building. The man was storming the bastille.

Eventually Barrise and Steele found other jobs. Tommy hooked on at East Carolina as an assistant; Mike got a similar job at Belmont Abbey. Bill Goldring found employment as an SID at Indiana State, Larry Bird's alma mater. But it wasn't before he got turned down for the head publicity job of the Sun Belt Conference.

Actually Bill wasn't turned down. Commissioner Vic Bubas wanted to hire him and Bill had received some strong support from several other schools in the conference. But JU, showing its true colors, blackballed him. They had enough key alumni put pressure on the right people to overrule the conference vote.

One more thing about my staff. They all worked under a severe handicap at JU. To illustrate how poor the JU basketball program was upon my arrival in March of 1978 can best be demonstrated by the salary structure of my staff.

I had been given $13,500 to split five ways. Thom Shannon and Barrise were my full-time assistants and each received $3,000. John Baldwin, a local part-time assistant coach, got $1,000. So did Mike Steele, who was then a graduate assistant coach. That left $4,000 for Bill Goldring and $1,000 for our trainer. It was really bush league. I told each of them that in lieu of money, I was giving them an opportunity to work at the Division I level.

So much for making it to the top level of college basketball.

By June of 1981, however, I was wondering if I would ever make it back to *any* league again. For months I had applied for just about any and every college coaching job which had come open. I struck out each time. Some of the schools I tried included Richmond, Creighton, Rhode Island and Manhattan. I really thought I had a solid shot at landing the Manhattan job but it never panned out. I was told I was among the final five candidates for the job but no one ever bothered to interview me.

Frankly, I couldn't blame any school AD from shying away from Tates Locke. Even before the pending suit against Jacksonville University most schools had been afraid of me, afraid of my image. I'm sure many of them had felt I had cheated again and got caught at JU.

I was broke...or damn near close to being broke. I had some bills that had to be paid and I needed to earn some money to put food on the table for Nancy and the kids. I had moved back in with Nancy, to our home in the city. It was a comfortable place: four bedrooms, 24,000 square foot lot, three baths and a family room. It was worth around $60,000, or $5,000 less than the beach home. If I didn't find work real soon, one of them would have to be put up for sale. Maybe both.

I received a couple of offers for jobs in the East and North. I didn't want to go to Boston or Detroit to work in heavy equipment sales, however, but then again I couldn't afford to be *too* selective because we were getting further and further into debt. Fortunately friends had loaned us a few dollars, but that amount wasn't going to last us forever.

Finally I accepted a job in Jacksonville at the Mayport Naval shipyards as a clerk. I worked the 3 p.m. to midnight shift, seven days a week and overtime on the weekends. I made five dollars an hour, barely enough to pay our bills. I did a bunch of odd jobs on the Lexington, an aircraft carrier, but mostly I was a watchman, guarding a particular section of the ship. In five weeks at Mayport I did a lot of watching...and thinking.

I wondered what the next season might have brought at JU. We had made an adjustment in our recruiting and I finally thought we had made it over the hump. When it came to recruiting in-state prospects, we were at a disadvantage at JU because unlike the other schools in Florida, we could not offer a kid new facilities. And we weren't offering them money. So there was two strikes against us.

Sometimes it became a bitter pill to swallow. For instance, I remember the time a contact of mine presented me with 15 violations of NCAA rules by another school in Florida. It was in the autumn of 1980 when I discussed the charges with President Kinne and asked her what she planned to do about it.

A day later she called me, saying, "Let's drop the issue. We've got too many members of our Board of Trustees who are graduates of that respective institution." That was her answer. I didn't want to fool with the allegations myself, so I handed them over to our school president, figuring she would take *some* kind of action.

But she washed her hands of it. That bothered me.

It shouldn't have been too surprising, in that many people involved in collegiate athletics don't want to deal in realities. That hurts too much. For instance, there were members of the JU Boosters Club who didn't think it was fashionable the way I talked to my players. It's funny, but some of the people who criticized me were some of the same individuals who had tried to shove cheating money down my throat.

One member in particular stands out. Not only was he a booster, but a member of the trustees. It happened in the summer of 1980. We were at a party at Doug Milne's beach house when this individual got himself quite intoxicated and offered me money to go out and buy JU some ballplayers. I don't recall the exact amount he offered, but it was somewhere between $5,000 to $10,000. I told him I didn't want any part of it, that I was not going to get involved in anything like that ever again.

My answer didn't sit too well with him.

I have to laugh at those kinds of incidents, especially since coming to the University of Nevada at Las Vegas to work under head coach Jerry Tarkanian. UNLV has been placed on probation in the past by the NCAA and Jerry's battles with the governing body of college basketball are legendary. I know a lot of people are smirking at the thought of me hooking up with Tark. If I told them I've yet to see a dollar bill pass hands or a player receive a free car, well, few folks would believe me.

But then, people are going to believe what they want. I learned that at Clemson and again at JU. I know most folks are probably saying, "There goes Frank and Jesse riding again."

Let them.

Coming out to Nevada was not a bad move. Hell, it was the *only* move I had when you face the facts. I know I've got a long road back, but I'm only 45 years old and I still want to play for the national title some day. That's been my dream ever since I got into coaching at West Point and it's still my goal today.

The way I figure it, I fell off the train awhile back and then I got bumped off again in Florida. Now, I'm back on the right track again.

jacksonville university **NEWS**

OFFICE OF PUBLIC RELATIONS / JACKSONVILLE, FLORIDA 32211 / 904-744-3950

Mary Anne Rogers, Director of Public Relations
Jerry L. Gantt, Assistant Director of Public Relations

April 1, 1981

COACH LOCKE RESIGNS AS JU BASKETBALL COACH

FOR IMMEDIATE RELEASE:

Tates Locke, Head Basketball Coach at Jacksonville University, submitted his resignation to the school's Board of Trustees late Wednesday afternoon.

Coach Locke joined Jacksonville University in 1978 and has been very instrumental in making the program one with national recognition.

The Coach's resignation is effective immediately. There was no indication given as to his future plans.

Robert T. Shircliff, Chairman of the Board, announced that a search committee will be appointed immediately to seek a replacement.

-30-

JACKSONVILLE UNIVERSITY IS AN AFFIRMATIVE ACTION/EQUAL EMPLOYMENT OPPORTUNITY INSTITUTION.

jacksonville university NEWS

OFFICE OF PUBLIC RELATIONS / JACKSONVILLE, FLORIDA 32211 / 904-744-3950

Mary Anne Rogers, Director of Public Relations
Jerry L. Gantt, Assistant Director of Public Relations

April 2, 1981

TATES LOCKE TERMINATED AT JU

FOR IMMEDIATE RELEASE:

Representatives of Jacksonville University, including President
Frances B. Kinne, Chairman of the Board Robert T. Shircliff, and Doug
Milne, Chairman of the Intercollegiate Athletic Committee of the
Trustees, had a long and detailed discussion with Coach Locke yesterday
about his management, direction, and leadership of the basketball
program and his compliance with the management policy and directions of
the University in areas unrelated to the performance of the team or the
coaching of the team.

At the conclusion of that meeting it was determined that Coach
Locke would not be continuing as head basketball coach, and it was
the clear understanding of the Jacksonville University officials that
he had resigned. It was with surprise that they later learned that
Coach Locke claimed not to have submitted his resignation, and
accordingly, today President Kinne took action to terminate his services
as head basketball coach effective immediately.

Steps are now being taken to appoint a search committee to seek
a replacement. President Kinne reaffirmed the University's commitment
to develop and maintain a/major college basketball program.
                              ⟨high quality⟩

-30-

3
BRANDED FOR LIFE

To understand how I gained my outlaw reputation and tag of "Cheater" perhaps it is best to flip back to the final weeks of my five-year coaching career at Clemson University. There is a scene in there at Littlejohn Coliseum which pretty much puts the situation into perspective.

The 1974-75 season had been somewhat of a disaster throughout December and into much of January. Until then we were struggling but around mid-January the team showed signs of starting to play well. It was a very talented team, as talented a team as there was in the Atlantic Coast Conference at that time, including defending national champion North Carolina State, which had forward David Thompson back as a senior.

We started by winning three of our first four contests, losing by one point at home against Penn in the finals of the IPTAY Invitational. Then we got blown away at Louisville, 80-75 and lost by four points and two points to La Salle and Dayton in the Dayton Invitational. That made our record 3-4. We split two games in the Pillsbury Classic, losing in the finals to Minnesota by 66-52. We finished 1974 at 5-5 when we beat Florida Southern by 19 points on the last day of the year.

It was time to get into our conference schedule. We got away from the gate quickly, defeating Virginia by 18 points. Then we fell back into our old habits, losing on the road to North Carolina, 74-72, and to Duke, 75-72. On the morning of January 16 we were 6-7 and I was feeling rather sick. Make that pissed off.

All of a sudden, our fortunes began to change. We came home to beat Wake Forest, 80-77, then downed Maryland, 83-82. We went to Virginia and beat them by 10 points. Home court victories against North Carolina, 80-72, and The Citadel made it five straight. N. C. State cooled us off at its place, but we came back to beat Wake, Duke and Georgia State. We came into our February 22 home game with N. C. State with a 14-8 record. We were peaking just at the right time with the league tournament scheduled in two weeks. On top of all this, the national polls had us ranked as high as 14th in the nation. Yeah, I was feeling mighty good.

I'll never forget the scene that evening at Littlejohn. For days everyone in the state was talking about Clemson basketball. Having the defending national champs coming into our little snakepit gym was going to be exciting. It was going to be a great challenge for all our players, one of the great contests in the history of our school.

All kinds of rumors had been following our team around concerning a pending NCAA investigation. It had been going on for months; every city we played in there were signs and newspaper articles written about us. We were the "Bad Guys", the rebels of college basketball. It was a well talked about subject even in tiny Clemson.

It was kind of a carnival or circus in town. The people there really didn't know how to take this instant success. For so many years, Clemson had been the doormat of the ACC. In fact, when I began coaching the Tigers in 1970-71, the school had recorded a winning record in only three seasons since joining the ACC as a charter member in 1954.

Like I said, this carnival atmosphere seemed to blot out the gray cloud which was hanging over Clemson basketball. At least for the moment. Game time was 3 p.m. against State but as early as two hours before tapoff people were outside in the Coliseum parking lot, picnicking and tailgating just like they did before a football game.

Obviously, I knew our team was going to be on the spot that day but I was getting used to the pressure by now. Not only the pressure on the court, but off the floor as well. My assistant coaches, Charlie Harrison, Bill Clendinen and graduate assistant Tommy Gaither and myself were never fully aware of what was going on concerning the NCAA investigation. The administration obviously knew more about the investigation than we did, but they were always assuring us that everything was fine. "We are going to fight this thing and we'll be with you to the bitter end," was a favorite phrase used.

It had gotten to the point where Clemson president, Dr. Robert C. Edwards (I called him R.C.) was making a number of visits to our locker room to assure me and my kids that everything was going to be alright. On a number of these visits R.C. was heavily under the influence of alcohol. He would come in and say, "Fellows, forget about what you read in the papers. Forget about what's happening. Forget this...don't worry about it. We're gonna fight this thing."

27

Then R.C. would always look over to me and say, "Coach, you're our man. Don't worry about a thing. We will take them to the highest courts." His favorite saying was, "We're gonna brand some noses."

Well, before our game against N.C. State, Edwards made one of his visits to our locker room for a pep talk. I always cordially brought him inside, which may have been a mistake on my part. But I thought this was the least I could do to protect the interest of everyone, particularly my staff and myself.

R.C. began to give one of his famous monologue speeches.

"Forget those things and these people on Tobacco Road," he began. "They're the ones who are responsible for all this... for us getting all these bad reports. I'm tellin' you, we're gonna fight this to the bitter end. You coaches are sound...you're in our system. You're our coaches..."

Edwards started to repeat himself. A lot of the words were slurred. Finally, from the back of the room, one of our players—I think it was our big forward Wayne Croft—had heard enough.

"Coach,"shouted Croft, "will you please get him out of here."

After this scene, we went out there before a capacity crowd of 11,000 and played as fine a basketball game as I ever had a team play. We blew State out of the Coliseum, winning 92-70.

We just killed them. We fouled out David Thompson. Tree Rollins, our 7-1 center, was overwhelming. And Skip Wise, one of the sweetest shooters you'd ever want to see, had an outstanding game. Tree got 12 points and Skip threw in 30. Jo Jo Bethea had one of his best offensive games of the season with 13 points and Stan Rome chipped in with 11. It was a totally satisfying victory, making us 15-8. We had won nine of our last 10 games. It should have been one of the happiest moments of my career, walking off the court and shaking hands with State coach Norm Sloan.

Only it wasn't so great.

As I was leaving the court, I happened to look up into the stands. I couldn't believe what I saw. There was President Edwards, along with athletic director Bill McLellan and a bunch of other administrators, dancing in the aisles. Their noses were painted with tiny orange tiger paws. Fluorescent orange tiger paws. They were up there dancing around, slapping each other on the back and acting like idiots. It was a scene out of a Mardi Gras.

As I watched more closely, Charlie Harrison approached. I put my arm around my assistant coach as we headed to the locker room. "Charlie, it's over baby. They don't need us anymore. It's history. Piss on the fire and call in the dogs. The hunt is over."

Charlie didn't quite understand. He asked me about what I had said later that evening.

"Coach, what do you mean it's over?" he asked. "You mean to tell me we're finished here at Clemson?"

"I think so, Charlie. We're gonna be sacrificial pigs when this NCAA investigation is through."

You see, the Clemson athletic department and alumni had pretty much achieved what they were after when they hired me in 1970. They had waited years and years for this—to be nationally ranked, to win a major game. They had sought to be competitive, not only during the regular season, but in the ACC tournament as well. And we had brought them to that level. They saw a winning basketball program as a way out of the pit which the school had been buried in for so many years. People at Clemson had always felt stepped on. Second class, if you will.

Now they were first class. Now they were winners. And when the shit hit the fan from the NCAA investigation, Tates Locke and his staff were going to be the pigeons.

I could see the avalanche about to bury me but there was nothing I could do but sit back and wait for it. It was like standing before a firing squad, blindfolded, and waiting for them to squeeze that trigger.

4
WELCOME TO
THE ACC, COACH

To begin with, I really didn't have any idea what I was letting myself in for when I signed my first contract with Clemson on March 18, 1970. I had no idea the ACC would be such a vicious jungle, on and off the court. Those are wars that are fought in that league...and sometimes they shoot real bullets.

Maybe I was a little naive, but more than likely I was a little too sure of myself. Of my methods. Clemson had experienced only three winning seasons since 1954 and all three had come under my predecessor, Bobby Roberts, who had resigned after his eighth squad went 7-19 in 1969-70. I came to Clemson thinking with a little hard work on defense and some breaks in recruiting we'd have the Tigers back to a respectable, if not a championship, level.

I'm big on teaching my players defense. My two teams at West Point went 40-15 and finished third in the NIT each season. It was no coincidence that both the 1963-64 and 1964-65 teams were ranked in the Top 10 in defense nationally. It had been pretty much the same at Miami of Ohio, where I coached from 1966 to 1970, compiling a 56-42 record. Once we made it to the NIT and another time we played in the NCAA tournament. All four of my squads at Miami were ranked in the Top 10 nationally in defense.

At those schools I had coached very deliberately...and mostly legally. Except for a few technicalities, I didn't bend the NCAA rulebook. Probably the only rule I broke—I like to say stretched—was one which dealt with working out players in the summer months. Individually, not as a team. By working with a player, one-on-one, I might be able to help him correct a flaw in his game. Maybe we'd work on pivoting. Or getting a better first step off the dribble when driving to the basket. Little things like that. It was my belief such individual attention would enable the player to be better mechanically prepared when practice began in the fall.

Technically, I was in violation of NCAA rules, which prohibit coaches from directly working with any player during the off-season. One player and one coach in the same gym playing basketball is a violation. To say the least, it is an absurd rule.

Especially at a military school such as West Point, where there was a definite limitation as to the amount of time a player could spend to develop his athletic skills. Therefore a player at Army was deficient in his overall skills compared to other Division I players and it was a tremendous disadvantage when you asked these players to go head-to-head against some of the very best talent in the country. The same held true at Miami. We were playing a national schedule all the time and, in order to cope, we *had* to offset this disadvantage with individual work in the summertime. We had our Miami players go through two-hour routines every day in the summer. There was nothing secretive about these drills but, nevertheless, the bottom line was we were cheating.

Look, I know we were violating the rules but how could I ask my kids to go up against people like Donnie May or Dan Issel or Rick Mount, game after game, without a little extra work? Naturally, when I came to Clemson, I figured the summer sessions would be the only rule-bending we would need to do. I felt if I was to give up my time and lend my so-called expertise to try and help a player that we would eventually overcome all the hurdles in the ACC.

In other words, by doing just a tiny bit of rule-bending, we could hopefully avoid some of the real nastiness—the illegal recruiting stories you hear and read about so often—which was going on in college basketball at the time.

I wasn't blind to what some of the other schools in this country were doing to attract top high school prospects to their campus. Remember I went to Indian Hill High School in Cincinnati and later graduated and played ball myself at Ohio Wesleyan University. I had grown up in the shadows of the University of Cincinnati when they recruited Oscar Robertson. I knew what had gone down at schools such as Bradley, Wichita, North Texas State and Memphis State.

When people ask me how I was able to recruit at Miami without cheating I point to the triangle in high school basketball—right there in the Ohio Valley. You've got Kentucky, Ohio and Indiana right before your eyes. We would get castoffs from the Big Ten, the Southeastern Conference and the Missouri Valley. The Mid-American Conference, and particularly Miami,

31

reaped the benefits of players overlooked by the major conferences.

We didn't have to cheat at Miami. The players we got merely needed extra work. The guards in our league were as good as anyone, players like Howard Komives and Phil Lumpkin, both of whom made it into the NBA. We had some great individual talents in that league.

So did the ACC. No one had to tell me about the talent in that league. Still, I felt if I worked a little harder than the next coach I could survive just by spending a little extra coaching time in the summer. Or so I thought.

First impressions can be misleading and the first impression my 1970-71 Clemson team gave people *was* misleading. We won three of our first four games that season, losing only to Vanderbilt.

Then we tackled the ACC. Boy, did we ever get pummeled.

We opened against Frank McGuire's South Carolina team and lost by 28 points. Then Georgia Tech dropped us by 18 in a non-conference game, followed by a 10-point loss to Virginia, a four-point setback against Maryland and a 20-point embarrassment against North Carolina. Welcome to the ACC.

After a 3-1 start we proceeded to lose eight of our nine games. It was very fitting that our 9-17 season ended at the hands of Dean Smith's team in the opening round of the ACC tournament in Greensboro, N.C. North Carolina almost doubled the score on us, 76-41.

Looking back, I knew by the eighth game we were in for trouble. I realized by then that all the teaching, dedication and that kind of stuff were not going to help tiny Clemson climb the mountain. Hell, it didn't look like we'd make it up to the first ledge.

One major problem at Clemson was quite obvious: We didn't have enough black ballplayers. I mean *good* black players. Oh, we had two on the squad in 1970-71 but neither was a super prospect. And for us to get one of the blue chip blacks, it appeared almost impossible. We would have to drag a kid all the way through the ACC, since a southern black did not qualify for the 800 college boards.

To get immediate help I had to turn my efforts toward recruiting junior college players. Black, white or green. Just find me someone who could play. I needed some guards badly, especially a point guard. Finally I found one, a white youngster, Bo Hawkins. Bo was 5-10 and had played high school ball in Louisville at Lindsey Wilson Junior High School, averaging 12 points a game. Bo did a nice job for us in 1970-71 but he never would have been on our team had it not been for an assist from the Clemson administration.

Bo, you, see, didn't have the grades to get into Clemson. But thanks to the school registrar and an academic advisor in the athletic department all that was changed.

Quite frankly, that incident was only the beginning of my troubles at

Clemson. Sneaking Bo Hawkins into Clemson was the worst thing I had ever allowed myself to be party to in my years of college coaching. But we were desperate. We were having trouble signing anybody because of my late arrival in the recruiting season. We had to get *somebody*. At the time, changing the grades of Bo Hawkins seemed like a major crime; within two years, it would be minor compared to the stunts we pulled.

For instance, I remember an episode involving Jeff Reisinger in the spring of 1972. Reisinger was an All-American 6-6 forward out of Anderson Junior College. He had played for a Kingston, Ohio high school championship team and had been set to attend Ohio University. However, his board scores fell short, so we caught him at the last minute and sent him to Anderson, S. C. to improve his marks before bringing him to Clemson.

Unfortunately, Jeff wasn't any better of a student at Anderson than he had been in high school. In order to make him eligible at Clemson we had to get him enough quality points and grade points. That meant taking a correspondence course...or rather, someone else taking it for Jeff. It was a math course, I believe. There was no way he could pass it on his own.

We got him some help. One of my assistant coaches had his daughter take the course for Reisinger. She got him a "B" and we got ourselves a player.

Recruiting at Clemson in those first few years was never easy and was made more difficult because of the college board restrictions. When I first arrived on campus, school administrators told me to hang on, that in another year we would not have to fool with the 800 college board requirement. As a result of that promise, my staff and I recruited in the fall of 1970 with that idea in mind. We brought in some of the greatest talent—not necessarily academic talent mind you—in the country, reaching out to all parts of Florida, as far west as St. Louis and as far north as Baltimore.

At one particular Clemson football game that fall, we had 11 or 12 of the best high school players in the country lined up across our 50-yard line for halftime introductions. Prospects like Fessor Leonard and Clyde Mayes, both of whom later attended Furman, Rick Suttle of St. Louis, who played at Kansas, Allen Murphy, who attended Louisville, and Sam McCants, who attended Oral Roberts

Big Wayne Croft of Bamberg, South Carolina was also in that group, a 225-pound youngster who we began recruiting during his junior season at Bamberg-Erhardt high school. Although I had never seen the 6-9 Croft play, I had been told by several good sources that Croft was the *best* high school prospect in the state of South Carolina.

Bamberg is what we call "low country", located not far from Orangeburg. It is a quiet mill town with a low economic, social income. Family folk live in Bamberg. Anyway, to show Wayne we were interested in him, we invited the kid to our summer basketball camp in 1970. We paid his way, which was in direct violation of NCAA rules. That summer, we had paid the way for a lot of prospects to come to our camp. I mean, if you're going to break the rules, you might as well do it up big.

The recruitment of Croft was soft at first. We went the same route as any other school, going to his home for frequent visits. We would take him to a Clemson football game and pay a lot of attention to him. Anybody who was anybody was after Wayne Croft. It was obvious he would have the necessary 800 on his college boards, he was white and he was big. And he could play. Wayne had been coached very well in high school, a rare feat in itself back in those days in South Carolina.

We visited Croft as often as possible. We serviced him right. By Christmas, it became apparent we weren't the only school servicing him right. Everytime you went into the Croft house there were gifts, cakes, food. All that kind of stuff poor folk need.

The Crofts were a large family. Mary Croft worked; John Croft was a former truck driver but was now disabled. They lived in a run down frame house and they had rent problems. They had electrical problems, too. It was always cold inside that house.

To partially understand what we were up against in our recruitment of Wayne Croft you first have to understand how easy it was at the time for out-of-state schools to come into an economically depressed state like South Carolina and recruit a prospect. It was really a piece of cake to come in and grab a kid out of South Carolina in the early 1970s.

We learned early that enticing Croft wasn't going to be an easy job. A couple dozen schools were sending him groceries, turkeys and other foods. I finally saw we had two choices: either go in there and do the job illegally or get the hell out and forget about Wayne Croft. There could be no in between. I told members of the Clemson alumni the Croft family needed help.

They agreed with me.

The first thing we did was make a priority list of things we could do without getting our hands dirty. That was number one on our list. Try and do it legally if at all possible. A second point was to get active with HUD, to get that government group to help the Crofts with their housing situation. Next was transportation. Maybe we could get the Crofts a car.

Wayne's family was driving around in an old Valiant. I don't even think they make those things anymore. The entire family would load into that run down car and go places. If it held out, fine. If it didn't they would walk the rest of the way. That's how badly that car functioned.

The heating in the Croft residence was brutal. No wonder heat couldn't stay inside. You could look down through the floors and see under the house. That's how large the gaps were in between the floor boards. It was not surprising they used over 100 gallons of oil every month.

The whole picture was pretty sad and we got involved to help them out. It was petty stuff in the beginning, nothing compared to what we would do later. Sometimes it would get to me watching how we had gotten involved. I'd see us do the Crofts a favor, then sit back and watch another school come in and top our favor. It was like our opponents were saying, 'Can you beat this?' Like I said before, I had never been involved in something like this. It was crazy...but still we continued.

Wayne was a hard recruit. It got to the point where we would have to fly into his home once every week. I would be at practice and get a phone call or just get bad vibes and we'd send an assistant coach to his home to see if everything was alright. We also had some local help in Bamberg, our own spy who watched Wayne almost 24 hours a day.

I don't know what we would have done without little Alvin Cooler. God bless Alvin. He was a little fellow, about 5-4. We called him Tooley. Cooler was the team manager of Croft's basketball squad and someone who Wayne would confide in when he was troubled by the pressures of his recruitment. Tooley became our most important contact; he relayed to us all of Wayne's innermost thoughts, kept me posted daily. Tooley would let me know specifically who had come into Bamberg to visit with Wayne and what they had offered him or his family.

Wayne had difficulty discussing the situation with his father. Ol' John Croft was a swashbuckling, beer drinking guy who could hold his liquor. He could disarrange a bar in five minutes, that's how tough he was. I respect him even today. I mean, I would go fishing with John tomorrow. I really like him, but shit, I wouldn't fight that guy with an army because once he got drinking nobody was going to kill him.

Wayne's father seemed to be waiting for the best deal to come along. Unlike his wife—Mary wouldn't succumb to anything dishonest—ol' John was waiting for the best train to come through. In an hour's time he might change his mind three times depending on the offers. The mother just wanted her son to be happy—she was a good Christian lady. But dad...well, like I said he was going with the best ship he could find. It was scary.

It got so bad that we had to fly into Bamberg by private plane just about once a week to shore things up with Wayne. To let him know that we wanted him to attend Clemson. And when we weren't at his house, somebody else was knocking at his door. When we were with Wayne, we'd try to get him off to the side and make him understand the value of people. I tried to show him how some of the other schools were only using his family to get to him. For instance, North Carolina State had one alum who would drive into Wayne's town in a big Cadillac. He was from Lumberton, N.C. and he'd come in there and spread all this bullshit. Thanks to Cooler, we knew every time the guy stepped foot in town. In truth, people like this N.C. State alumnus were abusing the Croft family. In a sense the Crofts were being prostituted.

I really believe Wayne understood that but the pressure of going home every night to a cold house and seeing that old clunker car in the driveway must have gotten to him. I know it would have gotten to me.

By now, it was late into February and the season was pretty much shot. We were practicing for the conference tournament coming up in a few weeks in Greensboro. I knew we weren't going to fool anybody in that one. We were going to get our doors blown off in the ACC tournament. I knew it, my staff knew it and the kids must have realized it, too. Besides, my mind wasn't on the tournament. We were working on next season. We needed players...people like Wayne Croft.

One day after practice I got a long distance telephone call. It was from Wayne. He was crying. He was really upset about something, so I told him to hang in there and we'd get to his home as soon as we could. I hung up the phone and headed for our private plane, which had been provided by a member of the Clemson alumni. En route to Bamberg is when I made one of the biggest decisions of my coaching career.

I decided that Clemson had to prostitute itself in order to get Wayne Croft.

In other words, we were going to join the other crooks in the college ranks. The cheaters, the rest of the whores who were competing for young high school talent. We would go to Wayne and give him our best deal. I felt we didn't have any other choice. It was either cheat...or forget about signing Wayne.

That's when the idea of the fishing trip came to my mind.

My assistants and I decided the best way to reach Wayne and his father—especially the old man—was to isolate them from the other schools. John Croft loved to fish and drink, and not necessarily in that order, so we decided to work toward the old man. Alvin Cooler had told me about John Croft's interest in fishing. Alvin knew everything, which is why we later offered him a full scholarship to Clemson to become our team manager, in charge of the equipment and things of that nature. Alvin was a real gem.

So was Cliff Malpass, my assistant coach in charge of the freshman team. Cliff had joined our staff in late May of 1970 after serving as an assistant coach at The Citadel. He was a former baseball shortstop in the Yankees' minor league organization. A real good man, one of the best assistants I have ever had. It was Cliff who had shadowed Croft for so many months and naturally he was my choice to keep Wayne and his dad company on the fishing trip. Oh yeah, Alvin Cooler went along for added insurance.

I set the entire trip up by telephone. Got them boats, fishing tackle and a lodge to stay at along Lake Santee. It was a remote little fishing hole and I knew nobody would find them there. And I also knew the crappies were biting at this time of the year, so Wayne and his dad would have the fish they wanted. All the booze, too. We loaded up the car with alcohol and beer. We wanted to be sure that John Croft was happy.

I think one of the more humorous sidelights to the venture was the selection of the campsite. North Carolina State was one of several schools in the hunt for Croft, so it became a primary goal to shield Wayne away from State's influence. Ironically, when we were looking around for a lodge at Lake Santee to stash the Crofts, we settled on a place owned by a couple of State graduates. I couldn't believe it when they agreed to rent the place to us. That has always tickled me. I mean here we were living right under the cat's paw, eating away at his heels.

Well, we finally got the Crofts on their way to Lake Santee. It was a beautiful week for fishing and drinking. When they arrived, I had instructed Cliff to hide the car keys. There wasn't anyone who was going to get out of there for a whole week.

I felt pretty comfortable at the ACC tournament knowing we had the Crofts right where we wanted them. As expected, North Carolina ripped us apart in the opening round of the tournament, 76-41, but I was doing plenty of smiling deep inside. All the while the tournament was being played, I'd look up at the clock in the Greensboro Coliseum and was content knowing the Crofts were out on the lake fishing. It was a great feeling knowing exactly where your number one prospect was every minute of the day. I don't know if the N. C. State coach ever caught on to what we did, but I do know that some friends of his told me they spent the whole week looking for Wayne.

We finally signed Croft to a full scholarship later that spring, but not before we got another scare. I mean a real scare.

My assistant Bill Clendinen and I had planned to take the Croft family to the state high school all-star game in Columbia that spring. The plans called for me to meet Bill and the Crofts in Columbia; Bill was going to pick them up in Bamberg. It appeared to be very simple.

When Bill arrived at the Croft residence, Mary and the children were ready but John had still not come back from getting a haircut in town. He had been gone for five hours. So Bill loaded Mary and the kids into the car and they set out to find John.

As we found out later, John had stopped off at a couple saloons along the way and also visted the town pool hall. He was in there bragging about how his boy was going to be playing in the state all-star game. Time had gotten away from him and he was hours late getting to the barber shop. About the time Bill and the rest of the Crofts were driving down Main Street in Bamberg—I think that's the only street in that little town—John Croft was getting a haircut and a shave. He must have been looking out the front window when Bill's car went by because the next thing my assistant knew there was John Croft standing out in the middle of the street with shaving cream on his face, still covered with the barber's smock. He was screaming at Clendinen to come back.

Mary Croft took one look at her husband and told Bill to keep on going. Columbia was an hour and a half drive and she wasn't about to wait for him, especially knowing the foul mood he would be in after hitting those saloons. So Clendinen kept on going.

Of course, I'm in Columbia and I don't know *any* of this. I'm sitting there before the game, basking in the festivities, when I get paged over the Coliseum public address system. "Coach Locke, please pick up the nearest phone." So I did. It was John Croft.

John proceeded to tell me he had a 45 revolver and the next time he saw me or my assistant or anybody who was in the car which left Bamberg without him he was going to shoot first and ask questions later. He added he would start by shooting Clendinen.

You can imagine my thoughts. Needless to say, I spent the rest of the afternoon on the telephone with John Croft, trying to settle him down. I never saw one minute of the all-star game. Finally, it got to the point where he said he wasn't going to shoot *me*, but I wasn't so sure about Clendinen, who had to drive the Croft family home after the game. I knew damn well *I* wasn't going back in that car.

Sometime in the second half, I finally located Clendinen and Mary Croft and told her of John's threats. Then I said to Bill, "We can't let the family go back home tonight. He'll kill them. Every last one."

Mary Croft wouldn't hear of it. She said she would go back and straighten out the situation with her old man...and she wanted me to come along. I said, 'Wait a minute, Mary. There's a lot of things I'll do to get your boy to come to Clemson but getting shot isn't one of them.'

And I didn't go back there.

After the ballgame, I visited with Wayne in the locker room. He had played a great ballgame (I was told) and had been named the Most Valuable Player. I told Wayne what had happened with his father and he said not to worry about a thing, just have Bill Clendinen drop them off at the city limits and they'd walk home from there. Everything would be fine.

That is what we did. Or I should say Bill did. He took them back and nothing ever came of it. I guess by the time Mary and Wayne got back the old man was sleeping it off. He had forgotten all about it.

I don't think Bill Clendinen ever did, though. Talk about a guy being uptight driving back there? Come to think of it, I guess Bill had a pretty good reason.

5
GOD'S COUNTRY—
IF YOU'RE WHITE

My coaching career at Miami of Ohio was progressing quite well. In 1968-69 the Redskins had gone to the NCAA post-season tournament, quite an accomplishment since we had been picked to finish fifth in the Mid-American Conference in many pre-season polls.

I guess that just shows you what some sportswriters know. Oh well, at least they were nice enough to select me as conference Coach of the Year.

We came back in 1969-70 with another respectable team, one that finished with a 16-8 record, enough to earn a spot in the NIT. It was while preparing my team for that post-season tournament in Madison Square Garden that I received a telephone call from Clemson University athletic director Frank Howard.

Howard was a native of Barlow Bend, Alabama, a bigger-than-life, bald-headed southern gentlemen who had put Clemson football on the map. When he stepped down as head football coach in December of 1969 it ended the longest tenure of any college football coach in the nation at the time. After 30 years and 165 victories, I guess Frank had paced the sidelines long enough. Plus, in recent years he had doubled as the athletic director, so I imagine at age 61 he figured one hat was enough to wear.

When Clemson basketball coach Bobby Roberts resigned February 11, Howard began an immediate search for a successor. He called friends and associates but it wasn't until he contacted The Baron, University of Kentucky head basketball coach Adolph Rupp, that my name popped into the picture. Being endorsed by a living legend never hurts and I'm sure Coach Rupp's recommendation got me in the front door of Frank Howard's office. Before we went to the NIT, Howard called and asked me to fly to Clemson for an interview.

Of course, I accepted the offer.

The idea of coaching a major college basketball program in the prestigious Atlantic Coast Conference intrigued me and got my competitive juices flowing. I'm the kind of person who is always seeking a challenge; in fact, I find it emotionally stimulating when someone tells me there is no way I can succeed at something. You see, I believe if you put your heart into a project and work at it a little harder then the next guy nothing is impossible. So what if Clemson hadn't fielded a helluva lot of winning basketball teams in the last 20 years? That didn't bother me. If anything, it made me want to look into the opportunity more, much to the chagrin of my best friend, Bobby Knight, and some other close associates. They all warned me about what I was getting myself into but I didn't listen.

I flew to Clemson.

When you fly over Clemson, South Carolina—in fact, anywhere over the upper region of that state—you have to fall in love with the place. There's the beauty of the Blue Ridge Mountains and calmness of the crystal blue lakes which surround the campus. It's a place which is so much in order that it seems God meant for Clemson to be located exactly where it is on this earth.

The school, to their credit, knew the atmosphere was a selling point and they had me flown over the campus in a private plane. I guess it was while viewing the loveliness from that height that I decided I would take the coaching position if Howard made me an offer. From that plane I could see the entire athletic complex—Littlejohn Coliseum and the beautiful, spacious football stadium. Then there was the tradition of the ACC, one of the most difficult conferences in the country. Well, I saw all that before me and I thought to myself, 'Tates, obviously they care about having a winning basketball program here.' That clinched it. Later, when Frank Howard said "Would you?" I responded "When do I start?"

Looking back, I realize I made a terrible mistake by letting my emotions get the best of me. I had not really asked the administration a lot of hard questions about the direction of the program and I guess, because of my passive approach, I had painted them a picture of a fellow who could be easily swayed. Ultimately, that would lead to my undoing at Clemson.

Like I said, I was partially blindfolded. I had not examined closely enough the reasons why the Tigers' basketball program had dug itself into a deep hole all those years. To begin with, Clemson had no tradition of winning, but I assumed I could overcome that with hard work. Unfortunately, the other pitfalls which I would encounter would almost be impossible to overcome...especially if a coach had to follow the NCAA rulebook.

Probably the largest handicap was the general lack of support at Clemson for recruiting black athletes. There were virtually no blacks at Clemson University when I came in 1970. Realistically, I should not have been that surprised. After all, high schools in the South had only been integrated since 1968 and that section of the country was hardly prepared to welcome blacks into their colleges two years later.

It was the same feeling at Clemson, thanks to the attitude of the alumni and other heavy contributors to the athletic program. They preferred a lily white team, which didn't leave a basketball coach much room to wander in the ghetto playgrounds of the East, where many of the best high school talent was to be found. Again, had I looked into the situation more closely before accepting the job, I would have seen such prejudice at Clemson.

The fact that I was 33 years old when I came to Clemson was no excuse. I was far from being naive about racial unrest in the South. But it's one thing to hear about racial prejudice and another to actually experience it.

I had never heard the term "nigger" used until I got to Clemson. When I first heard it used it shocked me to death, probably because it dawned on me that an actual person was being referred to, not a people. It really shocked me. I had heard "nigra" before, but never "nigger". So here I was, falling in love with God's country in a little southern college town but not really knowing the standards or attitudes of the natives with whom I was dealing. Compounding the problem of the social acceptance of the black athlete was an even larger dilemma—the academic acceptance of the black athlete.

I had been told the ACC had an 800 minimum college board score requirement for all of its athletes. Clemson, itself, didn't have such a policy but the ACC did and as long as Clemson was in the conference it had to abide by that rule. About the only thing Clemson and University of South Carolina, the two ACC schools most affected by the rule, did to protest the 800 minimum was threaten to withdraw from the conference. I saw that as a chicken way out. One of the schools should have tested the rule in the courts. How that rule ever stayed out of the courts I'll never know. It was so wrong. But again, it was a classic example of the hypocrisy of the South and the ACC.

What all of this did, in terms of the Clemson basketball program, was make it practically impossible to recruit a kid from the South. Face the facts—most of the youngsters in that section of the country were not prepared academically to go into the ACC. So it became one big nightmare for us at Clemson those first couple seasons.

For us to attract the quality black athlete, even one who passed the 800 board score, was a tall order. By the time a youngster from New York or Ohio or somewhere else in the East had been dragged all the way through the ACC, by the time he had a chance to see life at the other campuses, Clemson had two chances of getting him—slim and none. By being the southernmost school in the league we were geographically the last stop along the trail. Toss in our far inferior social standards, for blacks that is, and you had one big mess.

In 1970 you still had two sides of the street in Clemson, one for whites and the other for "niggers". It appalled me. I had only seen something like it once before in my life, during the summer I worked at Delta State University. The administration assured me the situation would change, that within a year the 800 board requirement would be dropped, thus enabling Clemson to attract more blacks to our campus...both students and athletes. In the meantime, I was told to hang in there for another season, then go out and start recruiting the best black athletes I could find east of the Mississippi.

But there was a catch. How, I thought to myself many a night, are we going to recruit a quality black athlete when we can't even show him a decent time socially when he visits our campus? It was a realistic question. I knew under the present circumstances a black kid visiting Clemson would laugh at our campus atmosphere. We'd only be kidding ourselves and wasting money. Then I hit upon an idea: Why not create a *phony* social atmosphere for the blacks?

Enter the era of the Phony Black Fraternity.

Boy, did we do a great job of acting on this one. The bunch of us should have won Academy Awards. Hell, we took these old, quonset hut houses some of the married students used to live in and fixed them up, turning them into "fraternity houses" where we could entertain our black recruits.

The charade didn't stop there...it only began.

We would go into surrounding communities, places like Seneca, Anderson and Greenville, and bring back to campus as many black high school students, seniors mostly, as we could find. Then it would appear as if Clemson was integrated on the weekends. We went out and hired bands, held dances and even provided transportation to and from the social activities.

In 1970 the student enrollment at Clemson was 8,900. Maybe one half of one percent—and that's a high estimate—was black. However, you would never be able to tell by looking at one of our weekend fraternity functions. You'd have thought we were a branch school of Grambling. Yes sir. Reality didn't hit until Monday morning, when you could look all around campus and see mostly white faces. During the weekdays, life was back to normal at Clemson University.

I'll never forget this one fall weekend. We had invited a slew of hot-shot high school basketball players to visit our campus. On Saturday they attended a football game...there must have been 50,000 fans watching when these kids walked to the 50-yard line at halftime to get introduced, one by one. Well, a couple days later I had to speak at an IPTAY boosters club meeting in nearby Greenwood. Many of those people had been at the football game and seen only two white faces among the halftime guests. I knew it had bothered some and I was waiting for someone to mention the subject. Sure enough, a loud voice from the back of the room raised the question.

"How many of dem niggers you plan on signing?" the one fellow drawled. The room fell silent, waiting for my response.

"As many of them that want to come to Clemson," I shot back.

Now it *really* got quiet.

I couldn't ignore the facts, however. And the facts were our Phony Black Fraternity looked about as legitimate as a three dollar bill. You could see right through the damn thing. I knew we weren't fooling any of our black guests for one minute, either. Hell, you'd walk into the dances and there would be all these blacks sitting around the room. Nobody was talking! Where I grew up in Batesville, Indiana you could smell stuff when it wasn't right...and this black fraternity smelled. I mean, those people were as uncomfortable attending those parties as I was watching them in attendance. Enough was enough.

I can laugh at the situation now. I mean, here we had spent all this effort and money to create this so-called "beautiful experience" for these people and there was nothing. Absolutely nothing.

The abolishment of the Phony Black Fraternity only led to bigger troubles. We still had the same problem before us—how to present a social atmosphere which was meaningful to our black prospects, one that would entice them enough to attend Clemson. It came down to one simple fact: if we couldn't create a social atmosphere on campus for our black students, then we had to do something to lead them into a social involvement off campus, in places like Greenville. Trouble was, how was a poor black youngster going to get to Greenville?

By car, of course.

Which explains why we had to start providing some of our better black athletes with a set of wheels.

During my five years at Clemson I helped many of my players out with their personal transportation but only once did I actually purchase an automobile for a player. I use the word 'automobile' rather loosely since the car I bought for Jo Jo Bethea was ready for a junkyard. Jo Jo was a talented black guard, a kid who had transferred to Clemson from Anderson Junior College in time for the 1973-74 season. He was one of two outstanding blacks we recruited that previous spring, the other being Tree Rollins. The 1967 Plymouth I bought Bethea cost $1,023 and was part of the "package" we put on him. We never said we were buying a kid, we used the phrase "put a 'package' or 'program' on him".

I still cry from laughing so hard when I think about Jo Jo's ol' junker car and how the NCAA sent a bunch of investigators to our campus during the 1974-75 season to find out about the cars we had allegedly given our players. They must have been shocked when Jo Jo led them to a local trade school where he had been overhauling the engine. That junker was a mess. The NCAA investigators saw this old car up on cinder blocks and one of them looked at Jo Jo and said, "You mean *that* is the car they gave you?" I can imagine the shocked look on their faces, questioning some kid about a piece of junk.

Not all the cars were junk. A couple players had newer models. Wayne Rollins, the 7-1 center who we called Tree, had a Monte Carlo compliments of an alumnus. Skip Wise, our star freshman guard from Baltimore, also had a car given to him. I stayed completely out of who was given what merchandise but I knew these kids weren't buying it with their own money.

That's one of the cute ways a college coach learns to stay clean. The smart ones stay away from those kind of illegal transactions. They let someone in the boosters club or a prominent alumnus take care of it. That way they can look you straight in the eye and say "I'm clean". Technically, they are.

The only thing I know for fact is Jo Jo and Tree, my two black recruits in 1973, were taken care of by someone from Clemson. Mostly it was Rollins who got the royal treatment...or should I say it was his mother, Wilma Robinson. I know Tree got a car and received a monthly allowance, of which he saw very little. Most of the money was mailed to his mom's home.

Like I mentioned before, I spent a lot of my personal money to provide players with personal transportation. I would say in five years I must have spent between $40,000 to $50,000, buying them plane tickets to go home for the holidays, money for car rentals, money for gasoline. Things like that. Spending money. It was $20 here and $30 there. It didn't seem like a week went by when some player didn't need an extra buck.

You might wonder where I was getting the money. Good question, since at $20,000 a year I was the lowest paid coach in the ACC. I started at $20,000 in 1970 and was making $23,000 when I left in 1975. Some improvement, huh? Actually the money for my players came directly out of profits from my summer basketball camp. Without that money we wouldn't have survived. None of us, me, my assistants or my players. I made about $20,000 off the camp but I always split it four ways with my assistants. In that way, each assistant made enough to bring their annual salary to $20,000 or more. What was left after paying my assistants I reserved for my players.

Sometimes there were good reasons to spend money on the kids, like the time during the 1973-74 season. It was in December and we were going to Pittsburgh to play in the Steel Bowl Tournament. Tree Rollins arrived at the airport in a light windbreaker—he didn't own a winter coat. So on that trip I bought Tree a coat with my own money. I think it cost $100. It wasn't anything super, but the kid needed a coat! What was I going to do, let my star center get pneumonia?

I took a similar, personal view about the holidays. Most of my players had no money or transportation to get them home for Thanksgiving or Christmas. I believe this is a time of the year a college kid should be with family if at all possible, so I'd slip them $50 or $100, whatever it took to get them home for a day or two. But that was a criminal offense according to the NCAA rulebook. According to *my* rulebook, it would be more criminal not to help out a youngster in that kind of situation.

There was another source of money for players—from a secret slush fund.

The fund was originated by three or four die-hard alums and set up in a bank in Columbia. Any check written needed two signatures. The monies for the fund were raised by a conglomerate of people soliciting to other Clemson supporters secretively. There were some real heavyweights involved in this scheme, mostly football people.

Their original intent was to supplement this secret account by the sale of Tiger Paw rags, a gimmick similar to the Pittsburgh Steelers' Terrible Towel. Because several of the boosters had connections with local textile plants, the rags could be produced quite economically, about 15 cents apiece. Then the rags were sold for two dollars each, with a dollar going back into the slush fund to repay monies being loaned to athletes. In this way, the money was untraceable. It was cash. That money was to be deposited in a Columbia bank, but whether it ever was I don't know.

I never got into the logistics of it. All I know is that each athlete's family, or the ones which were receiving help, were given enough money each month to meet the car payments. The players never saw the money. It was sent to their parents.

While I never got involved in the mechanics of the fund, I do know it existed because several of my friends had been approached and asked to make a contribution. They did not want to get involved, either, and called me to find out what was going on. I would tell them what I knew and assure them any contribution would be greatly appreciated. That was the extent of my role, but I think some of my friends lost respect for me, figuring I was endorsing the scheme. I know that is how it must have appeared to them.

Actually, I never used the slush fund as an inducement to attract a ballplayer to Clemson. I would never tell a kid that "if you come to Clemson you'll get so much money." On the other hand, let's be realistic. I was never that good of a recruiter to lure a kid like Tree Rollins away from, say a University of Kentucky. No, to get Rollins to come to Clemson over about six other top schools we had to be doing *something* under the table. I knew some of the things and I had a good idea about some others, but Tree and I never spent much time discussing the subject. Again, I just didn't want to know.

With the possible exception of our recruitment of Moses Malone, I don't believe the promises of money, cars and clothing were made to our kids when they came to visit Clemson. Most of the offers were made in the privacy of their homes. With Malone it was different. I know there would be times Moses would be out of my sight on a recruiting trip for three or four hours. During that time he would be visiting with members of the Clemson alumni.

Particularly this one alumnus. B.C. Inabinet was in the homes of every one of our top prospects and he swarmed all over Malone. He was a super salesman and I admit, I solicited this guy to help me. Let me say I didn't discourage him. He was one of the best salesmen I've ever known, armed with promises of grandeur that were incredible.

Our players had a monthly spending allowance and received a number of gifts from various sources. Items like radios, stereos and items of that nature. I don't know who got what. In some cases the appliances were put in their parents' homes. Sometimes I'm not so sure it wasn't the mothers of the players who were doing the asking for these gifts.

I kept out of the details, but I knew what was coming down. I knew my players were being taken care of and that's all that counted. The kids never came to me for the heavy stuff, just some spare cash. And I gave it to them out of my pocket.

One thing I want to make perfectly clear—IPTAY, the booster group which raises money for Clemson's athletic scholarships—was not involved in the secret slush fund. IPTAY (which used to stand for I pay ten dollars a year) was and is a very fine organization, a group numbering over 10,000 which annually raises $500,000. At least those were the numbers in my final season at Clemson.

There were some members of IPTAY who got involved in the slush fund. Inabinet, the ringleader, was a member of IPTAY but he was acting on his own. B. C. owns one of the largest maintenance services in the Southeast, Defender Industries of Columbia, South Carolina. He's a master salesman.

There were two other fellows heavily involved as well, Junius Smith of Rocky Mount, North Carolina and Phil Chappell of Columbia. Both were members of the Clemson alumni and were forbidden by the NCAA to partake in any school fund-raising activities during the three-year probation. B.C. was told to do the same but I'm sure that was a joke. I doubt very seriously if Inabinet disassociated himself from Clemson athletics even for three weeks.

As for the slush fund, as far as I know it never really amounted to anything. It was lacking in funds and some of the heavy contributors got hurt financially. A couple of them were decent folks. I remember this one guy had to mortgage his house and sell his business because he got in debt over the slush fund.

A lot of their troubles might have been avoided—and perhaps the NCAA investigation, too—if they had worked the arrangement differently. It was ridiculous for them to put all their money into one fund. It would have made more sense for each "heavyweight alumnus" to fund an individual player. One guy would have gotten Rollins, another Wise, another Rome and so on. That way if anybody shot a gun the entire group wouldn't have to answer for all the problems.

That's exactly how some schools hide from the NCAA—they spread out and make 'em look in 25 different directions for clues. Clemson didn't do this...it was stupid.

And Clemson got caught.

Tates Locke in a 1966 photo.

Tates, during his reign as head coach at West Point.

Bobby Knight, assistant coach under Locke for two years at West Point.

Miami of Ohio team captain Tom Slater and Head Coach Tates Locke (1969).

Frank Howard during his tenure as
head football coach at Clemson.(Above)

Howard resigns as Clemson's
football coach. (Left)

B. C. Inabinet, pictured as a former Clemson tackle, during his senior season.

Bill Clendinen, Assistant Coach,
Clemson basketball.

Charlie Harrison, Assistant Coach,
Clemson basketball.

George Hill, Assistant Coach,
Clemson basketball.

Alvin Cooler, Clemson basketball manager.

The brothers find a "place" (the phony black fraternity) to get together. From left to right: Peanut Martin, Colon Abraham, and Tree Rollins.

Littlejohn Coliseum—Home of the Clemson Tigers.

6
TAKING TO THE AIR

Following a horrendous first season when we went 9-17, we jumped off to a 6-2 record the next season, opening with victories over Purdue, Holy Cross and Auburn. That was followed by conference wins against Maryland and Duke. Then we regressed. We lost 14 of the next 18 games and finished a disappointing 10-16. Sure, it was a one game improvement over '70-71 but coaches don't stay employed very long with those kind of improvements.

Offensively our '71-72 squad was well-balanced—center Dave Angel, forwards Denny Odle and Mike Browning and guard Terrell Suit all averaged between 11 and 14 points—but lacking in depth. However, there was help on the way. Van Gregg, a 6-3 guard-forward out of Columbus, Ohio, Wayne Croft and 6-7 forward Ricky Hunt, from the much celebrated D.C. area high school De Matha, all performed well for the freshman team or Cub squad as we called them. Gregg averaged 24 points, Croft 18 and Hunt 15. So we knew we had three solid players on the way to the varsity in 1972-73 but in college basketball you can never be sure of having too much depth.

In other words, you should recruit hard *every* spring.

By the fall of 1971 it had become obvious to me that we had to make an adjustment in our method of recruiting on the national level. We were still being inhibited from recruiting southern blacks because of the 800 college board minimum restriction so we had to go off in another direction. In an effort to get a student-athlete who could qualify academically, we had to go into states like Ohio, New York, Illinois, Indiana and Washington, D.C.

In order to do that we had to sell Clemson University long distance. And I don't mean using Ma Bell, either. No, we decided we would have to take to the air.

It was not easy.

Clemson University was not exactly your household name in college basketball. In fact, a lot of people in this country had never even heard of the school. Oh, people knew about the ACC when we mentioned it in our recruiting sales pitch but they also asked if you had a map. I had better things to do than play geography teacher.

So we decided to put together our own fleet of private airplanes, privately owned craft which were big enough to transport recruits, their coaches and in some cases even the parents to our campus. If you brought the group in by private plane, which so many colleges do today, it is difficult to keep track of the number of flights a recruit receives, much to the dissatisfaction of the NCAA police force.

This was our first fling at reaching out and bringing Clemson closer to others. We had done it earlier with Ricky Hunt and also in the spring of 1972 when we went to New York to sign Charlie Rogers, a powerful 6-8, 220-pound forward. That spring we also recruited Bruce Harman of Pittsburgh, a 6-0 guard, and two Ohio kids, Tim Capehart and Scott Conant. There were some notable failures, too. We lost Otho Tucker to the University of Illinois and Mitch Kupchak to the University of North Carolina.

Kupchak was a clean recruit. By that I mean we didn't put a "program" on him or fly him back and forth illegally to our campus from his home in Long Island. In fact, we had gone to the Island to look at Lindenhurst's Rogers and ended up watching both Charlie and Mitch since they often played against each other. I don't think we did a bad job of recruiting Kupchak, it's just that North Carolina and coach Dean Smith did an excellent job. It didn't hurt matters that Dean had an established program. A winning tradition has a lot to do with recruiting when most everything else is equal.

One change we did make in our recruiting tactics was a shift toward bringing in prospects during the spring, not during football season. We worked hard at getting our prospects to attend our games in February or early March, when the weather in South Carolina is quite nice. Believe me, that is a selling point to a youngster coming out of the cold Midwest or East. Another selling point became our spring basketball banquet. We would find a big name speaker for a guest—I believe we invited Adolph Rupp in 1972 —and fly in our prospects for a wild weekend of partying.

Although the 1972-73 season again showed a statistical improvement in the won-loss column, to 12-14, we still had won only four ACC games, two of which were over Virginia. However, it was an improvement and the best record posted by a Tiger team since the 1966-67 season.

Van Gregg led us in scoring with a 13.6 average, followed by Jeff

Reisinger, our junior college "under the table" find. Reisinger was the only other starter in double figures at 11.7. Angel, Browing and Suit all dropped off in offensive production to figures of 8.8, 8.5 and 7.1 points respectively. Croft was somewhat disappointing with a 4.8 scoring mark and Charlie Rogers saw action in just two games because of a broken ankle. Ricky Hunt, who had put on too much weight, was another major disappointment, contributing 2.5 points a contest.

Our other recruits of 1972 were not any better. In fact, as a group, Capehart, Harman and Conant averaged under seven points. Conant made one field goal all season and Harman but three. Get the picture? Needless to say, there was some pressure on us to come through with some prospects in the 1973 recruiting campaign.

Therefore we decided to intensify our talent hunt. Until then we had failed to attract that one special player who could turn around our program and, who in turn, would attract other solid players. David Thompson had done just that for North Carolina State, and people like Tom McMillen and Len Elmore had put Maryland into the Top Twenty. We had to find someone along those lines.

In December of 1972 I received a telephone call which would change our fortunes. It was from my chief assistant Bill Clendinen, who was excited about a tall, lean center he had been stalking in Cordele, Georgia. Wayne "Tree" Rollins was his name and Bill swore the kid could lead Clemson basketball out of the woods.

"Tates, I think we gotta kid who could be a franchise for us," I remember Bill gushing over the phone. "I think we can go in and do a number on him. There's not a whole lot of schools recruiting him right now."

Bill was right. Only about two small southern schools had inquired about Tree Rollins up to that point. Tree was a friendly, quiet young man whose performances had been overlooked at Crisp County High School in Cordele. For instance, in one game against Albany High School Rollins scored 34 points, brought down 29 rebounds and blocked 16 shots. In another contest, he blocked the opponents' first five shots. Rollins was huge—he had sleeve and inseam lengths of 40 and 42 inches respectively. As the Clemson brochure would later point out, "Tree could have a bigger impact on the Clemson program than any other player in school history."

The author of that statement didn't know *how* true it would prove to be...and for reasons other than Tree's production on the court. I personally believe the NCAA's investigation into Clemson's recruiting activities began when we signed Rollins in the spring of 1973. Considering the schools we had beaten, it didn't take too many smarts to figure out Wayne came to Clemson for more than a handshake and a promise of a good education.

While Tree's reputation was a well-kept secret at the beginning of the

1972-73 season, it did not take long before universities such as Georgia, Jacksonville, Florida State, Auburn and Kentucky got into the picture. Even Hawaii made a run for his services. Hawaii has one very strong selling point: an airplane trip to its campus. How many 18-year-olds can resist an opportunity to fly to Honolulu?

Obviously, I knew we would have to go overboard to sign Rollins, so I prepared myself and staff and went to talk with some of the alumni. Some of the alums had come to me in the past and offered their assistance and I had always told them no. But this time I needed their help—and their money.

I told them we had found a player who we should "put a program on." I emphasized, though, that I wanted to be kept completely out of the picture. I wanted it to be where I would know nothing about any illegal inducements offered to Rollins. And that was the way it began...I was told very little.

In fact, to this day, the only things I know about his recruitment are from second-hand reports. After he came to school, Tree and I avoided discussing the subject. I never asked what he had received or expected to get in the future. I don't know why I never asked him. Well, maybe I do. I think deep inside I didn't want to discuss it with him because I was aware of some promises that had not been kept. Favors from the main man behind his recruitment, favors which B.C. Inabinet failed to deliver. That part was hard to swallow—the broken promises. I had learned about these from Wilma Robinson, Tree's mother, not from Wayne.

Some of the promises were astronomical. I'm sure Wilma wasn't lying. Just check the schools who were competing with Clemson. Kentucky, Florida State, Auburn, Hawaii. Come on! Clemson had to give Tree more than a 1973 Monte Carlo to spring him from that group. Bet on it.

As an example of the intensity which surrounded the recruitment of Rollins, there was an incident which took place at the Cordele airport which I'll never forget. It was right out of a Laurel and Hardy show.

It had been decided by our staff to bring Tree to our campus in early spring. Until then, I had avoided personal contact with Rollins; in fact, I only saw him play once in his senior season and that was at an all-star game. I had left the recruiting to my assistants and to the alumni. When we discussed final arrangements for Rollins' visit, it was decided we'd invite his mother, an aunt, a younger brother and some other relatives. I guess about six or seven from Tree's family would be flown to Clemson on B.C. Inabinet's private Aero Commander plane.

A date was set and we arranged to meet Wayne and his family at the tiny airport in Cordele. The plan called for them to wait outside the terminal and upon seeing our plane land to move quickly to the runway and board. That way we would only have to be on the ground momentarily and could avoid registering with airport officials. There would be no record of us having landed.

Of course, the best laid plans always have a way of finding a snag. Naturally, ours did.

Our plane arrived on schedule, but on the approach to the runway I became concerned. There was no sight of Tree or his family outside the terminal. The place was so small you couldn't help but spot them.

We decided to land anyway. Still no sign of the family. What could have happened, I thought? Then I found out. Coming in for a landing, not more than 500 feet away, was a private Lear jet. On the side of the craft were the initials FSU—Florida State University. Moments later the plane came to a stop on the runway. The door opened. Out popped Wilma, followed by Tree, an aunt, Tree's brother, who we called Little Tree, and the rest of the entourage. It was a real sight. Some of them were eating chicken or drinking from a champagne bottle. The two women had baskets of fruit, compliments of FSU coach Hugh Durham. Off they came, single file across the runway into our plane. It was going to be a doubleheader for the Rollins clan.

Next stop Clemson. All aboard.

Was that sick or what?

We finally arrived back in Clemson. It was a great weekend, a real social wingding. We took them to parties, one after another. And we danced. Wilma and I had a lot of fun together. We'd dance and really have a good time, but we always felt like we were in a fishbowl. During the entire time of Tree's recruitment, whenever Wilma and I were seen together at campus functions, or at an IPTAY meeting, it was as if we were being put on display. It was like, 'Look, we got a tall black guy and here's his mother and there is the coach.'

Wilma and I also had something else in common: our distrust of B.C. Inabinet. Sometimes we'd talk about some of the promises he had made to her. I'll tell you, B.C. was slick. I'd like to take credit for recruiting Tree and so would my assistants but it was B.C. who got the job done. He was the one who made it so we could be competitive.

When Tree finally signed in the spring, I don't think I've ever felt so relieved. We had accomplished what we had set out to do. We got us a franchise-type player, someone to put us over the hump. Tree was going to be our foundation, a youngster we could build our program around. After four years I felt good that something finally happened.

Little did I know that six months later the NCAA would begin looking into our program. It began that summer, when rumors circulated of a $40,000 to $100,000 package deal we made for Rollins. Again, beating the kind of competition we had faced only added fuel to such rumors. The schools which had been in the hunt for Tree were infamous for making illegal inducements to a prospect and you become guilty by association. But then, we *were* guilty. We had cheated and won.

What also hurt in subsequent months was B.C.'s public outbursts. During the next season, when we finished 14-12, and even in the 1974-75 season, when we had a 17-11 record and went to the NIT, Inabinet would occasionally pop off about his financial backing of Rollins.

I remember one time he told my assistant coach Charlie Harrison in a restaurant, "I got $40,000 tied up in that guy (Rollins) and Locke can't win with him." Statements like that, made publicly, were bound to get back into the hands of the wrong people. Eventually, it did.

I guess it was about the time of my fourth season when I began to feel badly about myself. I had gotten caught in a vicious circle. Small, innocent deceptions had led to bigger projects. I remember Harrison coming to me in October of 1973, not long after he had replaced George Hill on our staff. Charlie had seen Tree's car and wondered how the kid could afford one when he couldn't even afford a coat.

"Charlie, we got several members of the alumni to help him," I told Harrison.

"Tates, I don't know if that's right," returned Harrison. "Jesus, I just don't know if that's right."

"Charlie," I answered, "I did it because I just got tired of getting my ass beat in the ACC."

That is the truth. Simply, I had grown tired of losing. I didn't cheat because the Joneses did or because it made me a big man. I did it because I didn't want to get beat anymore. That's all.

My conscience bothered me. Here I was, the former coach of the United States Military Academy, bending the rulebook in every direction possible. I felt as if I had cheapened the game of basketball. I was also feeling badly about some of the kids who we had recruited into Clemson. Some of them weren't good kids and couldn't stand the pressures. They were succumbing to all sorts of social temptations.

But then so was I. I wasn't living a very exemplary life myself. I was taking all kinds of pills, drinking heavy and running the streets with women. I had never run the streets before. I wasn't happy with Tates Locke. I was ashamed of what I was doing. I was cheating my profession, cheating my family and cheating myself. I was in knots. My stomach felt like someone was hitting fungoes inside.

I kept on cheating. Common sense told me to get out, to start over, even if it meant leaving Clemson for another school. Foolishly, I didn't listen to my conscience.

Tree Rollins

7
MONEY GROWS
ON 'TREE'

There is big money to be made these days in professional basketball and I guess 7-1 Wayne 'Tree' Rollins is living proof of that. Before the 1980-81 season, Tree signed a five-year contract with the Atlanta Hawks of the NBA which totaled well over a million dollars.

In the NBA, which is a play-for-pay, big business type operation, the average salary is about $180,000. The players are entertainers, true pros, a term which separates them from the days when they played college ball. Back then they were called amateurs.

What a myth that has proven to be. Just ask Tree Rollins. He'll tell you about the pimping that goes on in the college ranks, the "amateur draft" a blue chip player goes through in his high school senior season. Al McGuire once called the whole scene "pimpish" and he was right. And the money being offered? It would make your head spin if you closely examined a college basketball program at many of the Top 50 schools. The coaches are involved, but most of the time their role is an indirect one. It's the aggressiveness on the part of the school's alumni, the guys with the thick wallets, and the permissiveness of the athletic department which contributes heavily to this deplorable situation.

"Tates is telling the truth," agreed Tree Rollins during a visit to his suburban Atlanta home in the spring of 1981. Rollins was Locke's biggest recruiting find in five seasons at Clemson and was completing his sophomore season when Locke was cut loose by the Tigers in March of 1975.

"I came to Clemson because of Tates...he was basically an honest guy. When I talked to coach Locke he was the only coach who recruited me who looked me square in the eye when he told me things. I was always brought up to look people straight in the eye and to respect those who did the same. You learn a lot about a person that way.

"Oh yeah, I know coach Locke knew I was being taken care of by the alumni, mostly by B.C. Inabinet, but he always stayed out of the financial end. He let B.C. cover that. Tates knew *something* was going on, but actually he probably didn't know half of what I was gettin'.

"If someone asked me to put a figure on what I got from B.C. and the rest of the alums over my career at Clemson, which began in 1973-74 and was completed in 1976-77, I guess the sum totaled about $60,000. I'd say that figure is very close, 'cause I was gettin' about $14,000 a year. That's countin' the money being paid for my Monte Carlo, the clothing allowances, gas money and pocket money.

"Clemson wasn't the only school which had offered me money if I played for them. There was a slew of schools. Back in the fall of 1972 and spring of '73 I was heavily recruited by Florida State, Kentucky, Georgia and Auburn, in addition to Clemson. And each school was offering me something different.

"For instance, Florida State talked to me about movin' my family near the school. They told me whatever I wanted or needed I would get. Those were their exact words. I mean, it got to be ridiculous. One night they brought the entire Florida State team up by plane to Cordele to watch me play a game. The *whole* team.

"Kentucky brought me to their campus in Lexington. Along the way we just *happened* to pass a thoroughbred horse farm. How ironic. Well, the one assistant coach who I was with points to one of the horses and says, 'Tree, if you come here one of these days you'll get one of them.' And there was more. They offered my mom and family a place to stay if I came to Kentucky...and whatever else was necessary. Oh, they did a lot of things to try and win me over.

"Another time they set me up with this good-looking black chick. Man, I couldn't handle that situation. I mean, here I was comin' out of little Crisp County High School, a tiny place in Cordele, Georgia. I wasn't used to that kind of treatment. I'm sure this girl was there just for sex. I didn't enjoy that situation at all.

"Auburn did things differently. They brought me in for a football game —Georgia was playin' Auburn. They knew my high school athletic director was hip on Auburn and I liked football, so they invited him and my basketball coach to come along on the trip. Here comes another irony: it just so happened a clothing factory outlet, Sewell Suit Company, was open after the game that Saturday and they took us over for a visit. Well, it was more than a visit, I guess. When we got there a guy made us a bunch of suits. We all came home with a lot of clothing.

"Then there was Clemson. This guy B.C. Inabinet was offering me every-thing. I got my '73 Monte Carlo thanks to him. And B.C. was flyin' my mom into many of our games the first couple seasons...things like that. He also promised her an apartment and a job in Clemson if she would encour-age me to go to school there. My parents were divorced and mom didn't want me to play ball too far from home, so that idea appealed to her.

"B.C. really got to my mom. He'd come to our house and spend a lot of time talkin' with her. Me, well I was trying to hide from B.C. a lot of the time. I guess I met him about seven times in all during my recruitment, even though coach (Bill) Clendinen did most of the recruiting. In fact, I only met coach Locke once, the time I flew to Clemson for my official visit. I came up there with my mom and brothers, all except Dennis, my older brother. He went fishing with some people at Clemson.

"I'll never forget the time we flew to Clemson on B.C.'s private plane. We had just gotten back from Florida State. Landed right on the same run-way not far away from the Clemson plane. We got out of one plane eating chicken and drinking champagne...I was drinking soda...and got right into B.C.'s plane. He had it all stocked with food and drinks. A great display.

"As far as my car was concerned, I knew B.C. was payin' for it but I never saw any of the money. It was always mailed to my mother, and she made the car payments. All I know is I never spent a cent on that car.

"You know, people ask me if I knew these favors were illegal. Sure I did, but all the other players around me in the league (ACC) were gettin' things for free, so I figured why shouldn't I take what's being handed to me. Believe me, Clemson wasn't the only school in the ACC doing it; I remem-ber Dean Smith's assistant coach tellin' me to come to North Carolina and they'd take care of me. Carolina made that very clear.

"Thinking about North Carolina brings to mind the time we were trying to recruit Phil Ford to Clemson. Ford was one of the best high school guards in the country, out of Rocky Mount, North Carolina. I got involved in his recruitment and so did B.C. It was a really *heavy* deal. We almost got Phil to come to Clemson. Toward the end, when he had just about picked Carolina, I asked Phil why he wasn't comin' to our place. I told him about the stuff they were givin' me. You know what he told me? He said, 'I got a better deal at Carolina.' Phil told me he was promised a blue and white van. He never got specific about the dollars, though.

"Phil wasn't the exception. He was the rule. It was going on all over the ACC. Look at the paved road they (North Carolina State) made to get to David Thompson's house. I know David was gettin' close to $30,000 a year from State countin' all the side stuff. And Kenny Carr (also of State) told me he was able to trade his car in for a new one every year.

"Like I said, I think all the schools cheat. Really. Once you reach the pros you sort of joke about it amongst yourselves. You say, 'Who got the best deal while they were in school?' We'd always ride Phil Ford about it, 'cause he joked about Clemson going on three years of probation. We used to tell Phil the only reason Carolina stayed off probation was Dean Smith had connections with the NCAA board. Phil would laugh and say, 'Yeah, you're right.'

"Phil even told me the last guy on Carolina's bench was being taken care of in some manner. I think only one guy at Carolina, Walter Davis, refused to admit he was gettin' something but you knew he had to be gettin' *something*. We all knew that.

"Then there was John Lucas of Maryland. Luke likes to talk all the time. He used to say Maryland had the greatest alumni in the league. 'We're the best taken care of team in the ACC' is how he put it. Tommy McMillen, a teammate of mine on the Hawks who also played at Maryland, would never talk directly about what he had gotten. Tommy would always tell us 'Maryland is straight' but he'd throw in a little grin just to let you know he was jokin'.

"Like I said before, I don't feel guilty for having taken those so-called inducements in college. It was just part of the game you played. It started back with the first school that tried to recruit me. Gardner-Webb College. They brought a car to my home and parked it out front. Told me it was mine if I signed with them.

"I sat down with my mom one day during my senior year and said, 'Mom, you know every team has offered me *something* to come to their school. What should I do? Should we go with the highest bidder?'

"You take a family like mine. One parent and six brothers. You see that kind of money being tossed around and you're bound to be vulnerable. I remember the time the University of Georgia was recruiting me. A guy who owned a lumber company was an alumnus of Georgia and they built my mom her home in Cordele for practically nothing. The final price was ridiculous...just because they thought I was going to their school. It turned out they changed coaches and I changed my mind.

"Actually, I liked Clemson and Coach Locke the best. It wasn't that hard of a decision. I trusted coach Locke and, of course, B.C. offering me all that extra stuff made it more attractive. The money he used to leave for me after a home game was unbelievable. It made you actually hate to play on the road. You see, after a home game we'd go to this steak house in Clemson, right down the street from the Holiday Inn. B.C. would always leave an envelope for us at the front register. I say us because Jo Jo Bethea was gettin' money, too. There would be $200 inside the envelope for each of us after most of those games.

"Clothing? I'd go to Columbia and visit B.C.'s tailor. I don't remember his name...I think his first name was Rajah, or something like that. He was a little Indian guy. He would outfit me in clothing every year, even in my senior season (1976-77) when Clemson was still in the second year of its three year probation. That didn't stop B.C. He was still payin' me my money and takin' care of some football players as well. Remember Bennie Cunningham? He was takin' care of Bennie, too.

"B.C. was there when you needed him. I remember when Colon Abraham came to Clemson. B.C. took care of Colon. I knew because Colon was my roommate. Sometimes we'd get low on our cash flow, maybe we'd be down to our last $10, and we'd hop in my car and drive to Columbia where B.C. lived. Every time we came to Columbia B.C. would have money for us and sometimes he'd put us up at a hotel, right down the road from his office.

"There was a restaurant right next door to the hotel and we'd always eat there because all you had to do was sign the tab and B.C. would pick it up. It was great. Sometimes you'd bring your girlfriend and some other friends and the entire tab was picked up.

"While B.C. was doing his best to keep us happy from a financial standpoint, coach Locke and his staff tried to make it comfortable for us socially. I don't mean he lined us up with chicks, but he tried to make life on campus more comfortable. Only it didn't work out that way. That phony black fraternity—the official name was the Student League of Black Identity —was a bust. They gave the SLBI this tiny building to hold dances and parties but only some of the black football players and soccer players used it. The basketball players usually went into Anderson or Greenville to party. Of course, we needed transportation. That's the reason we got cars.

"In my sophomore year we recruited this outstanding guard from Baltimore named Skip Wise. Honeydip Skip, we called him. He wore fancy clothes and drove a brand new Cougar. Skip was an outstanding offensive player, a great shooter from 30 feet. Some nights he couldn't miss. His habits off the court, though, left something to be desired.

"Skip was always gettin' into trouble with women. I mean the *type* of women he was datin'. He was going with this one chick, a woman-of-the-night type, and we always got on him about it. I think she charged him the first time but then Skip fell in love with her. I used to ask him, 'Man, how can you fall in love with a prostitute? How can you do that to us?' Skip would just laugh and walk away.

"Well, this one time he calls us in the middle of the night. Colon answers the phone and it's Skip. He's out of gas. He wants Colon to come get him. For a guy who was gettin' all this extra spending money, Skip was always running low on money, always running out of gas. It was amazing. I don't know where he was spending it.

"So Colon drives to the spot where Skip told him to meet him. No Skip, just the chick waitin' in the car. Skip had gotten tired of waiting and went off on foot to find gas. So there's Colon with Skip's girl and she's trying to come on with Colon. Just amazing. Colon told Skip about the scene later but he wouldn't believe it. That Skip, he wasn't too bright.

"We had other problems, too. All the money handed out to the black players caused some unrest with the white players. I think Wayne Croft and Van Gregg were the only whites being helped. Naturally there was some jealousy. Croft and Van got along well with the blacks. Come to think of it, we didn't have much friction with any whites *during* the season. It all occurred before or after the season when we scrimmaged. Then there would be all sorts of fighting.

"Stan Rome, who played forward for us and also was a good football player at the school, used to get in all kinds of fights with the whites. He was a good fighter. I wasn't, but I'd find myself getting into a couple. It got to the point where the white guys were taking cheap shots at the blacks. We'd come to the gym to play ball, but they'd come there for one reason: to try and hurt us. Finally we got hip to it and started inviting some big, black football players. Of course, they played on my side.

"What it had come down to, really, was a resentment of the preferential treatment given to the black basketball players. The money we got really pissed some of those white guys off. Come to think about it, I would have been pissed off as well if I had been in their shoes. But I was in my shoes and makin' 14 grand a year.

"It wasn't bad for only being an amateur."

8
A THREE RING CIRCUS

With the recruitment of Tree Rollins in the spring of 1973, Clemson began to get attention throughout the South. Tree opened up some doors for us...a lot of doors. When you recruit a 7-1 center, it almost automatically encourages other blue chip forwards and guards to look more closely at your school.

Tree, in a sense, had put Clemson basketball on the national map.

Along with Tree's recruitment, the ACC decided it would allow a school to bring in one player who did not have the minimum 800 college board score. This new legislation not only enabled us to recruit Rollins, but it aided our recruiting in the next two seasons.

The 1973-74 season, with Rollins as our freshman center, was quite successful, even though we got bounced in the first round of the ACC tournament by Virginia. Our 14-12 record was Clemson's first winning season in eight years. However, we still had a long way to go, since 11 of our victories had come against non-league rivals. Inside the ACC we had gone a poor 3-10.

So our next step was to start defeating some of the ACC schools, which is the strategy we mapped when we began recruiting in the fall of 1974.

We went after our first recruit, Stan Rome, very early, bringing him to Clemson for our IPTAY Christmas tournament. Stan loved the place and practically committed to us that first night. Rome was a great athlete, a two-sport All-American from Valdosta (Georgia) High School. He ran the 100-yard dash in 9.8 seconds, had over 4,000 yards in pass receiving in four years and finished his senior season in basketball with a 32-point,

20-rebound average. The kid made you drool, he was so good and it wasn't surprising *Parade Magazine* selected Rome as its top prep athlete in the nation. That's how good this kid was. Bear Bryant wanted Stan for his Alabama football team but Stan had decided he did not want to play football in college. But that didn't stop Alabama or Georgia from trying to change his mind.

In order to keep the pressure off this 6-5, 220-pound youngster, we "placed a program" on him. Of course, B. C. Inabinet was the main man behind the scheme, pulling the strings which got Stan a 1974 Monte Carlo worth $6,700.

Colon Abraham, a 6-6, 185 pounder from Darlington, South Carolina was the next prospect we sought. Colon was the most publicized high school player in the state that year, averaging 28 points and 14 rebounds for a Mayo High School team which went to the state finals.

Again, we placed a program on Colon, but it was a relatively light one. I don't know what it was, but it was light. B.C. took care of all the details, just like he did with Rome. In both cases, I would be told when to go into a home and visit with the prospect and the family, but I was kept out of the details as far as the money and extras were concerned. That was the way I wanted it handled.

Like I said, Colon came hard, but we finally signed him by April, shortly after getting Rome. We had the help we needed in the frontcourt, but we still needed a super guard.

Enter Skip Wise.

My assistant Charlie Harrison secured this one. Charlie had gone to Baltimore to watch the 6-4 Wise play for Dunbar High School and the two of them hit it off very well. In the end, it might have been that friendship which got us Wise.

The word had spread nationally about Wise early in the winter, He could shoot from 30 feet, possessed good fundamental ball control skills and was a winner—he had led Dunbar to three consecutive city championships and had been outstanding in a victory over Washington's De Matha High School, which had Adrian Dantley. According to the *New York Times,* Skip was rated the best guard in the nation by a panel of college coaches, including UCLA's John Wooden

So we made the big pitch for Skip and finally got him to attend a game against North Carolina State on February 23. At the time, Wise was considering "bids" from State, Maryland, Georgetown, Nevada Las Vegas and us. I think what impressed him about Clemson was we had a spot in the backcourt all ready for him...he wouldn't have to sit out and wait his turn. At Clemson, Skip knew he would be a starter right away.

He and Tree hit it off from the beginning, but then Skip got along well with everyone. He had a great personality, the kind of person everyone enjoyed. Skip Wise was a chameleon; he blended in regardless of the atmosphere. Skip could make you laugh and he could lift a guy's spirits even when he himself was feeling low. The only time Skip would ever *really* get down was when he didn't play well in a game. He was of the opinion that he should never have an off night.

Then too, coming to Clemson was a new experience socially. He had grown up in a Baltimore ghetto neighborhood and I was the first white coach he had ever had. It took awhile to gain his trust, but I think in the end he knew I'd walk the last mile for him. I just liked Skip, not only as a basketball player but also as a person.

He liked the attention you showed him, especially when he was in trouble, which was far too often. But I believe he liked the attention he got when he got himself into these predicaments. He'd come to my office and we'd talk. He loved to do that.

My own kids loved Skip and he was just great with them. They idolized him, not because he could put a ball in hoop, but because Skip was kind of a Pied Piper type. That's the way it was all around Clemson. People all over town, the kids especially, idolized him. From what I was told, it had been the same way back in Baltimore. Skip just had that magic about him. I mean, you can go back to Clemson today, six years after he left, and they still talk about the kid. He was, and still is, a legend at Clemson.

The most difficult adjustment Skip had to make at Clemson, as far as playing basketball was concerned, was dealing with me at our practices. Simply, Skip did not like being yelled at. Anyone who has ever played for me knows that I'm not exactly a soft-spoken guy at practice.

Beyond that, however, Skip was a coach's delight. I'll never forget how well he played for us in that 1974-75 season, especially in January and February. During those two months he secured his position on the All-ACC team. Amazingly, the kid did it by playing most of those games on the road. That's what was so impressive about Skip, which made him one of the premier guards in the league even though he was a freshman. A lot of big name players in the ACC make their reputations at home, not on the road. Not Skip. You knew that when he packed his bags, he was going to score at least 20 points that game. You could count on it...and we did.

Later on, after Skip left Clemson following my dismissal in 1975, he made a miserable mistake by signing a pro contract to play in the American Basketball Association. It was a miserable mistake. Not only did he get stiffed by the Baltimore Claws ownership, but the club folded during the exhibition season and he never played a game. Once Skip left Clemson I believe he knew he had made a mistake but by then it was too late. He was now a professional. After the Claws went under, Skip drifted into a few other NBA camps for tryouts but never caught on. His skills still needed refining, the kind of work he would have gotten in college.

Skip was left with nothing—no basketball and no education. It wasn't long before he got into trouble with the law, then into drugs. It was a sad, sad ending for a youngster who had more pure basketball talent than any kid I've ever coached.

People often ask me about my players at Clemson or Jacksonville and whether or not some were on drugs. I can never say no one *wasn't* on drugs. There are two things in coaching I will never swear to: one, that no one on my ballclub doesn't smoke or deal with drugs; two, that a player of mine never dumped a game. I'm talking about point-shaving.

Personally, I've always feared the dumpers. I mean, look at it this way, if a school can buy the services of a player for a certain amount of money and promises, what makes you think a gambler out on the street can't also buy him?

Back to the recruiting of 1974. That winter and early spring, in addition to getting Rome, Abraham and Wise we got ourselves another 6-6 forward, Jim Howell out of Williston, South Carolina. Overall, we brought in seven new faces but only four were top recruits. In fact, one of the others was a kid named Donnie Joy out of Baltimore. He had played at Dunbar High School with Wise and was a good friend. Basically we gave Donnie a partial scholarship just to make sure Skip didn't get homesick and leave. Donnie was to be Skip's caddy, his security blanket.

We didn't overlook anything.

Unfortunately, the recruit we went after the hardest that winter did not attend Clemson. We lost guard Phil Ford to Dean Smith and the University of North Carolina. Ford, who now plays for the Kansas City Kings, was a helluva coup for Dean. Can you imagine if we had had Ford and Skip Wise in the same backcourt in 1974-75? We might have won the ACC title and gone on to the very late rounds of the NCAA tournament. Now we'll never know.

We went after Ford very thoroughly, with great intensity. It was like a hunter stalking game in the woods. We used every trick we knew and we never let up.

It began in the third week of September, 1973 when we visited the Ford home in Rocky Mount, North Carolina. We met with Phil, his parents and his coach, Richard Hicks of Rocky Mount High School. Thereafter we would meet with them, call them or write to them regularly. Like almost every fourth day. In fact, between December 3 and January 24 we wrote at least 11 formal letters to Phil, his parents and coach Hicks. In the first two months of the high school season we saw Ford play 10 times. Eight visits were made by my assistant, Charlie Harrison, and the other two I made myself. By the end of the season I had seen Phil Ford play 10 times.

September 21, 1973

Mr. Richard Hicks
Head Basketball Coach
Rocky Mount Senior High School
Rocky Mount, North Carolina 27801

Dear Richard:

I sincerely appreciate your taking time out from your busy day to spend
some with us yesterday. I know this college recruiting will become a
headache to you, but I assure you that we will not contribute to any
inconvenience to you, Phil, or the community.

If ever I can do anything for you or your program, please do not hesitate
to give me a call. Best wishes for the season.

Sincerely,

Taylor Locke
Head Basketball Coach

TL:njj

September 21, 1973

Mr. Phil Ford, Jr.
1628 King Circle
Rocky Mount, North Carolina 27801

Dear Phil:

I sincerely appreciate your allowing us to come into your home yesterday and your taking time to spend with us. I was very impressed with you and your family.

I do not believe there is any doubt in your mind as to our sincerity in wanting you as a part of our program here at Clemson. You are an exceptional young man, and it would be an honor to be a part of your life in the next four or five years.

As I have told you, you are the one ingredient that our program is lacking. We do feel that our program here at Clemson is on the move and that you could definitely help us. I am also positive we could help you reach your goals both athletically and academically.

Thanks again for taking time to talk with us. I am looking forward to your visit. Best wishes for a fine season with much personal success.

Sincerely,

Taylor Locke
Head Basketball Coach

TL:njj

September 21, 1973

Mr. and Mrs. Phil Ford, Sr.
1628 King Circle
Rocky Mount, North Carolina 27801

Dear Mr. and Mrs. Ford:

Thank you very much for allowing us to come into your home yesterday. I sincerely appreciate your taking time to talk with us and your kind hospitality.

It is my hope that Phil will decide to attend Clemson for reasons in addition to the opportunity of being involved in our basketball program. He is a fine young man with a tremendous future, and it would be a sincere honor to be a part of his life during the next four or five years.

Thanks again for your generosity and for the friendship you have shown George. I am looking forward to your visit and seeing you again soon.

Sincerely,

Taylor Locke
Head Basketball Coach

TL:njj

December 3, 1973

Mr. Phil Ford, Sr.
1628 King Circle
Rocky Mount, North Carolina 27801

Dear Mr. Ford,

It was a pleasure to have the opportunity to meet with you on my recent
visit to Rocky Mount. As I mentioned to you in my conversation, we want
nothing more than for Phil to know about our continued interest in him,
and all of our visits to Rocky Mount will be just to reinforce this interest in him as a person and basketball player and having him next year as
a dominant force at Clemson University. I am glad that things are going
well for you and the family, and on my next visit I hope to have the opportunity to meet everyone in the Ford family.

I am sorry you missed the game at Sanderson. Phil's performance was the
greatest I have ever witnessed in a high school game. You certainly would
have been proud of him, Joe, and even the entire team. Phil is a winner
and a person of great character, and his performance against Sanderson exem-
plified not only his ability but the type of young man he is. Phil is a
young man that the entire school and community should be proud of.

Coach Hicks is an excellent man, and our misunderstanding was a lack of
communication. We now have a good rapport, and I think a good understanding
and friendship has developed. He did an excellent job during the Sanderson
game, and his poise and continued encouragement to the team exemplifies the
type of man and coach a school and community should be proud to have.

Best wishes to your family, and a special "hello" to Becky and Joe. I look
forward to seeing you on my next visit, and, should you have any questions,
please don't hesitate to call on me or Tates.

Sincerely,

Charles Harrison
Assistant Basketball Coach

CH/njj

December 3, 1973

Mr. Phil Ford
c/o Coach Richard Hicks
Rocky Mount Senior High School
Rocky Mount, North Carolina 27801

Dear Phil,

I want to congratulate you and your teammates on your wins over Tarboro and Sanderson. I was very impressed by everyone involved with your team, and your personal performance against Sanderson was the best individual performance I have ever seen in a high school game. Several times it would have been easy to quit, but the poise of everyone, including Coach Hicks, and the hustle paid off in what I know is a most gratifying win against a very good Sanderson ball team. Phil, you are a winner, and winners and competitors like you are what is needed to make any team not just good, but great. I know you, Joe, and the other players will continue to play as inspired as you did against Sanderson.

As I told you in Coach Hicks' office, we want you as a part of our program at Clemson, and I hope you realize that your presence along with Tree would be the makings of a new national power. Your presence would not be another addition to an already successful team, but the first or only great guard we have had at Clemson that will make us not only an ACC contender but a National power. Each visit that we make to see you will be a social visit to reinforce our interest in you. I look forward to seeing you, your Dad, and all of your family on my next visit, and we wish you continued success in all of your games.

Sincerely,

Charles Harrison
Assistant Basketball Coach

CH/njj

Enclosures

December 5, 1973

Mr. Richard Hicks
Head Basketball Coach
Rocky Mount Senior High School
Rocky Mount, North Carolina 27801

Dear Richard,

Congratulations are due to you and your kids for two excellent and impressive performances against Tarboro and Sanderson. I was very impressed with the entire team's effort and poise, especially in the Sanderson game where they could have quit but continued to hustle and refused to let the pressure get to them. You certainly did an excellent job in controlling the tempo in the last four minutes with well called time-outs and, after watching you on the bench, your poise seemed contagious and panic never seemed to enter into your mind or your players'. Congratulations to all of you.

I want to thank you for taking the time to speak with me. I am sorry if you misunderstood my inquisitive nature, but I had no idea what your rules were, and I did not want to violate any of them. I think we now have an understanding between us, and, regardless of how this thing with Phil ends, I hope we have established a lasting friendship.

Phil's performance at Sanderson was the best individual performance I have ever had the opportunity to witness. He was fantastic, and his teammates were just as great in those pressure packed minutes. You have not only a great team but an unbelievable group of young men. I do hope the people of Rocky Mount appreciate what they have representing them.

Thanks again for everything, and I look forward to seeing you again in the near future. Best of luck for continued success, and, when your big kid returns, I know that will make things even better for everyone. Be assured that all of the coaching staff at Clemson will work with you in all areas and comply with all of your requests, and, if we can ever be of any assistance to you or your program, don't hesitate to call on me, Tates, or any other staff member.

Sincerely,

Charles Harrison
Assistant Basketball Coach

CH/njj
P.S. Here is the calendar I promised you. Hopefully you will give us equal space on the walls of your office.

December 27, 1973

Mr. Phil Ford, Jr.
c/o Coach Richard Hicks
Rocky Mount Senior High School
Rocky Mount, North Carolina 27801

Dear Phil,

Just a note to congratulate you on your performance and win against Hillside.
You are having a great season thus far, and I hope it continues to go well
for all of you.

I also want to thank you for allowing me and Coach Harrison to have a few
minutes to talk with you after the game. I want to apologize for having
to come in on a game day, but, as I told you, I felt that it was time that
we sat down and had a serious conversation about my feelings about you
as a player and young man and how much I want to have you at Clemson next
year.

I will be seeing you often and very soon, and I want to thank you again
for taking the time to see me after the game. I am sure our relationship
has grown as a result of our meeting, but I promise you no other visits
will interfere with any more of your dates and personal fun that you deserve
and owe yourself, and I really appreciate your honesty and you coming over
to visit with me.

Best wishes to all of your family, and I look forward to seeing you all
in the very near future.

Sincerely,

Taylor Locke
Head Basketball Coach

TL/njj

P.S. Coach Harrison sends his best!

January 2, 1974

Mr. Phil Ford, Jr.
1628 King Circle
Rocky Mount, North Carolina 27801

Dear Phil,

Just a note to congratulate you, Joe, Boo, and your other teammates on
your performance during the Holiday Festival Tournament in Raleigh. It
was my pleasure to be at your semi-final game with Broughton, and, as usual,
I thoroughly enjoyed your performance. I am sorry that Kinston edged you
out for the championship, but all of you performed very well.

I look forward to meeting with you in the very near future, and Coach Locke
and I will continue to stay in touch.

Tree sends his regards. He has just won another MVP trophy as we beat
Furman for the Poinsettia Classic title. Continued luck and success to
you, Joe, the family, and the team for the new year.

Sincerely,

Charles Harrison
Assistant Basketball Coach

CH/njj

January 24, 1974

Mr. Phil Ford, Jr.
1628 King Circle
Rocky Mount, North Carolina 27801

Dear Phil,

I hope this note finds you and your ball club progressing rapidly.
The purpose of my writing at this time is to forward an article that
has found its way into some of the homes of young men like yourself.
If this article has not already reached your mailbox, I thought it
important that you see the type of recruiting tactics that are being
used by someone in the Tobacco Road area.

As to the validity of the statements in the article, I do not believe
that Clemson has anything to apologize for in this area. I showed the
article to Tree Rollins, and he really thought it was quite humorous.
It looks as though we are starting to bother some of the people in our
league if they have to stoop to such depths to influence a young man
about not going to Clemson.

I am looking forward to seeing you in the next couple of weeks. Good
luck to you and the ball club.

Sincerely,

Taylor Locke
Head Basketball Coach

TL/njj

Enclosure

Our recruitment of Ford contrasted sharply with the sales approach I had used the year before with Tree Rollins. Remember, I only saw Tree play in one game. In Ford's recruitment, however, I thought my presence at his games would be a factor in his ultimate decision. I knew Phil was a good kid, but he was getting a lot of attention from North Carolina, North Carolina State and Maryland. That's a heavy trio. Dean Smith, Norm Sloan (then coach at State) and Lefty Driesell can be three of the most persuasive people on this planet. Each is a great salesman in his own right, especially Lefty.

After our first visit with Phil in September I felt good about our chances of bringing him to Clemson. Naturally, we got B. C. Inabinet involved in the hunt, but in retrospect I think B. C. lost this one for us. B. C. simply came on too strong for Phil and his parents. I don't know what in the world B. C. offered them—later it was alleged he had offered Phil a new car, his parents new furniture and a cash bonus of $50,000—but I do know there was some money laid down in their home. I know the Fords have denied it publicly but I *saw* some of the money myself. Again, I don't know the final total, but I know some money crossed hands.

I also know that I almost got myself killed during this recruitment. On one occasion I made a trip into Rocky Mount in the worst storm I've ever flown in. Rain, wind, ice...you name it. I never saw the ground from the time we took off until the moment the wheels hit. I was never so scared in my life. Those are the risks involved, I guess. When you go after someone as talented as Phil Ford you take risks. Even the ultimate one.

There were some mistakes we made in our recruitment of Ford, but the most stupid one involved a coverup of a violation against our school which had been turned into the NCAA during its investigation.

On October 13, 1973 we had flown Phil Ford from his home to Clemson in B. C. Inabinet's private plane. At the same time, my assistant coach George Hill arranged for Junius Smith of Rocky Mount, a close friend of the Fords, to transport Phil's father by private automobile to Fayetteville, North Carolina at which point the father would be picked up by B. C.'s plane and flown with his son to Clemson.

Of course, when Clemson realized the transportation of a player and his parent by plane was in direct violation of NCAA rules, I was instructed by my athletic director, Bill McLellan, to fly back to Phil's home and have them sign an affidavit testifying Phil Ford, Sr. never made the trip in B.C.'s plane.

That coverup attempt only made things worse.

The Fords didn't like the idea. They called Dean Smith, who in turn advised the Fords to call ACC commissioner Bob James. I'm sure Dean didn't turn Clemson in himself. As a result of James' investigation into the matter, I was officially reprimanded and warned against repetition of such violations of recruiting legislation. Further, I was denied the privilege of contacting any prospective student-athletes outside the geographical limits of Clemson, South Carolina until August 1, 1975. I was allowed to respond to any telephone calls but I was prohibited from initiating calls to coaches or players for the purposes of recruitment.

Anyway, we lost Phil Ford but we didn't come away empty-handed. By April we had signed Rome, Abraham and Wise. We had three great prospects on the way and 1973-74 had gone fairly well, 14-12. For the first time since I had come to Clemson, I felt we had a realistic shot at competing for the ACC title in 1974-75. Life was looking pretty good.

But we weren't through yet. No siree. In April we got a tip that the most publicized high school player in the country wanted to take a look at Clemson. Naturally, I didn't ask any questions. I called Charlie Harrison and told him to meet me in Petersburg, Virginia.

We were going after Moses Malone.

October 15, 1974

President Robert C. Edwards
Clemson University
Clemson, S. C. 29631

Dear President Edwards:

In answer to the request of the Director of Athletics, Mr. Bill McLellan, I am attempting to reconstruct the recruiting violation incident involving Phil Ford Jr. of Rocky Mt., N.C.

On the weekend of October 13, 1973 (home football game with Virginia) the Clemson basketball staff had planned to entertain Phil Ford Jr. and through the efforts of Assistant Coach George Hill, arrangements were made to fly both Phil Ford Jr. and Phil Ford Sr. on a private plane to Clemson, S.C.

Mr. Ford Jr. was picked up in Rocky Mt., N.C., while Mr. Ford Sr. was picked up in Fayetteville, N.C., on the same private plane, having been transported to Fayetteville by Mr. Junius Smith of Rocky Mt., N.C.

The fact that we flew Phil Jr. was not in violation of N.C.A.A. rules, but a paid visit for Phil Sr. was in violation. I personally became aware of the situation after all plans were set and after the trip was in progress. However, there was still time to put a stop to the entire weekend, but I decided against it.

As the basketball season progressed it became apparent that we were going to have to bend additional rules to sign Phil Ford Jr., so we eliminated Clemson from consideration.

Only on one occasion did I attempt to call Phil Jr. after the middle of February and that attempt was made to see if there was any way we could clear ourselves of illegal involvement on the weekend of October 12 through 14th, 1973.

The entire Ford family encouraged me to come in at my convenience and said they would be willing to help us in any way they could. At the time, they were sincere about their concern over the possibility of

THE ATHLETIC DEPARTMENT OF CLEMSON UNIVERSITY

A Three Ring Circus

President Robert C. Edwards
Page 2
October 15, 1974

Clemson's getting in trouble with the N.C.A.A. I thanked them and told
them I appreciated their concern, but that there wasn't any immediate
problem.

On June 10th I called Mr. Ford Sr. and asked if I could fly in and
meet with him, Phil Jr., and Coach Richard Hicks, the high school coach
who had guided Phil in his decision to attend college.

They all agreed to meet with me on that day, Monday, June 10, 1974.
Mr. Hicks did not appear. During my visit in the home, I reconstructed
the problem created by our flying Mr. Ford in to Clemson and back to
Rocky Mount.

I proposed a possible solution to Mr. Ford Jr. & Sr. leaving a
facsimile of a recruiting expense form in their possession. This hand
designed facsimile was to be returned to me approved or not approved
by Phil Jr.

At the encouragement of Mr. Dean Smith, Mr. Ford Sr. turned the
form and his personal account of the weekend over to the N.C.A.A.
officials.

I am sincerely sorry for the embarrassment brought to the University
over this matter and can honestly say I would never condone such a
recruiting act again. However, if I were to be confronted again with
the decision of an attempt to cover up the mistake or not, with all
things being equal, I would. There were many considerations involved
in my decision, the main one being the hope that I could stop the
name of Clemson University from being involved.

I am hoping the reprimand can be & will be directed personally
at me and not the institution.

Sincerely,

Taylor O. Locke
Head Basketball Coach

bhm

85

WISE - ABRAHAM - ROME

List of "Programs" carried personally by coach Tates Locke in summer of 1974.

Skip Wise:	Car	Personal	Mother
June	$230	$100	$150
July	$230	$100	$150
August	$230	$100	$150
	$690	$300	$450

*All payments made by the 10th of the month.

Colon Abraham:	Car	Personal
June	$0	$100
July	$0	$100
August	$0 (purchased)	$100

*Payments all made by 10th of the month.

Stan Rome: Air travel to home: $97

Total payments spent on above three players in summer of 1974: $1,837

Additionally:
1. We made a $1,200 down payment on Skip Wise's car and the payments were $160 plus insurance.
2. B.C. Inabinet promised Mrs. Wise: (per month)

Rent	$68
Insur.	$36
Tel.	$25
Clothes	$20
	$149 per month

9
IN SEARCH
OF MOSES

In years before, there had been prospects like Wilt Chamberlain, Lew Alcindor (now Kareem Abdul-Jabbar), Jerry Lucas and Tom McMillen. Big, talented high school players. Pat Ewing, the youngster from Massachusetts signed by Georgetown University in 1981, is the latest to fit the billing.

It's amazing the kind of pedestal we coaches put these youngsters on, hailing them as being some kind of superior being. They are Superman without the cape.

Such was the publicity surrounding 6-11 Moses Malone in the spring of 1974 when Clemson University entered the sweepstakes for his services. Here was a talented player if there ever was one, a kid who had averaged 35 points and 25 rebounds a game during his senior season at Petersburg High School, not far from Richmond, Virginia. Forget about his scholastic average of "C", or the fact that he needed two "A's" in his last semester to get above a cumulative average of "C". You had to overlook that fact, just as you had to ignore the very real possibility that Malone might turn professional right out of high school. After all, the Utah Stars of the ABA didn't draft Moses just to waste a pick. The same thinking applied to Clemson; we weren't going to spend our time in Petersburg just to admire the scenery.

We were there, holed up in a hotel, for one reason only: to bring Moses Malone to Clemson.

Actually, we got into the hunt indirectly. Skip Wise, who we had just signed to a scholarship, was playing in an all-star game in Monticello, New York. Malone, who was still uncommitted to a school but who was considering about two dozen offers, was also playing in that prep classic in the Catskill Mountains. Fortunately for us, Skip and Malone hit it off extremely well in Monticello. Skip had told Moses about his decision to attend Clemson and I guess he noticed that Moses seemed to be quite receptive. When Skip mentioned this fact to me, I told him to "see if you can get involved."

Sure enough, Wise did.

Skip did some good talking. Moses listened. That quickly we had come out of nowhere to get into the hunt for Malone. In fact, very soon we would be among the final three schools, along with New Mexico and Maryland, that Moses had remaining on his list.

The recruitment of Malone on Clemson's behalf "officially" began with a visit to our campus on June 6. A few weeks before, a teacher from Malone's high school had called me and said Mo was somewhat interested in Clemson. I figured Wise had done his job, so I took it from there. I called Charlie Harrison back from his vacation to set up the visit by Malone. Charlie was surprised at the turn of events because he had been to the Malone home twice previously and had come away convinced Moses had ruled out Clemson.

So Mo arrived in Clemson at 6 p.m. on June 6. We checked him into the Holiday Inn, the hotel where we housed all of our recruits. Malone stayed there until June 9, leaving in mid-afternoon for a flight back to Petersburg.

Of course, me and Charlie Harrison were also on our way back to Petersburg. Little did we know we'd be there for 11 straight days. Yeah, I remember the Holiday Inn in Petersburg very well. In fact I even remember the room—number 407—we stayed in for that week and a half. You don't forget things like that when you're holed up in one place in a small city for 11 straight days. But like I mentioned before, you do what you have to do when a talent like Moses Malone is involved.

We weren't the only ones going to extremes to land Malone. Lefty Driesell and a couple of his assistants, Dave Pritchett and Howard White, were also holed up at the Holiday Inn. Maryland, I was told later, spent an estimated $20,000 during their recruitment of Malone.

Then there was John Whisenant, an assistant coach from New Mexico. He stayed at the Howard Johnson Motor Lodge across the street. He had been there for over two months when we got into town, arriving in late March after New Mexico had been eliminated in the NCAA tournament. Whisenant just up and moved to Petersburg, that's what he did. I guess the school figured it was better than flying back and forth across the country. Besides, Whisenant still managed to use the telephone and fly in and out of Petersburg often enough to get New Mexico three other prospects. And, most importantly, he got close to Malone. He had a good relationship with Mo.

Whisenant showed a lot of intensity during his recruitment of Mo but that's what it was going to take to land this kid. Mo was pretty quiet and fairly set in his ways. I think he really knew what he wanted but he was easily led. His mother Mary, for instance, wanted him to attend Maryland. Lefty had done a great selling job on her. Moses' coach, Robertnett "Pro" Hayes, was also offering Mo advice and he came down hard on Clemson. He didn't like us.

Then there was Malone's Uncle Charlie. Ol' Charlie Hudgins had a liking for Clemson and we, naturally, had a liking for Charlie. In fact, the very first night we arrived in Petersburg we made it a point to have Charlie Hudgins join us when we met with Mary Malone and Mo.

That was the same night Mo committed to Clemson.

"I'm gonna go to your school," Moses told me June 9. It's a statement I'll never forget for as long as I live.

Naturally, I was stunned. I mean, we were the Johnny Come Lately in the hunt. I did not know why, all of a sudden, this guy who was the greatest high school player in the country wanted to come to *my* school and play ball for *me*. It all happened so fast...I mean, there had to have been a ton of money laid on Mo somewhere along the line. There had to be, but to this day I don't know the specific amount. I swear I don't. But I knew Mo, or his family, had to have been offered something.

All I know is that right after Moses verbally committed to us he asked me if we could hide him out in a local motel until after his graduation, which was coming up very soon. "Just get me away from all these people," is the way Mo put it. As decision time drew near, he was getting an enormous amount of pressure from coaches, not to mention all that exposure from the media. It had gotten so bad that Malone set up a code system of knocks so he would know when friends were visiting his home.

The kid was buckling under the pressure and needed to get away and relax. So we helped him. Actually, we told Uncle Charlie to help him. I gave Uncle Charlie the money to pay for a hotel room. It was a flea bag place and I never even told Harrison about the financial part. You see, I didn't want any of my assistants to get hurt if it got out to the media. They couldn't be responsible for something they did not know.

We hid Mo away for two or three days. Got him some beer and stuff to eat. I think he brought along a woman, but I never saw the girl. Charlie Harrison told me he saw one. That's how I know.

Then Moses disappeared. Just vanished. He left the motel and nobody could find him for several days. Harrison finally caught up with him on a side street in Petersburg.

"Moses, I just want to find out what you're doing so I can stay here in town or go home," Harrison told me he said to Malone.

Talking to Mo wasn't very easy. It was like pulling teeth. Moses seemed confused. He told Harrison, "I don't know, man. I don't know, man. I don't have any idea what I'm gonna do."

We began to worry. One night we had arranged a meeting at his home at 241 Matthews Street, but he never appeared. We had set up the meeting to try and get back into the good graces of Mary Malone. She wasn't interested, either. When Mo failed to show Mary thought we had slipped her son something sly, some kind of illegal inducement. Now she was *really* against us.

So we went back to the Holiday Inn to continue our vigil. Meanwhile we'd hear from Uncle Charlie periodically. He'd say, "Don't worry, everything's alright. Everything's cool. Moses still wants to go to Clemson."

By now, some of the other schools had become also-rans. Schools such as Virginia Commonwealth, Houston, Detroit and Hawaii. Even Oral Roberts University had dropped out of the picture after using its ace in the hole—the old man himself, Oral Roberts. But Moses refused to bite.

Now it was down to just three schools—Clemson, Maryland and New Mexico.

Shit was flying everywhere. Every day, it seemed, a new rumor would find its way into print. There was a charge that Whisenant had loaned Moses a rental car belonging to New Mexico. One of the nastier stories had us—specifically me—handing $1,000 in cash to Uncle Charlie. I never gave that man a dime. Oh, I take it back—I did give him about $75 for Mo's hotel room. But that was it. You can draw your own conclusions as to where that $1,000 came from but if you ask me I'd say it was a safe guess B.C. Inabinet was at the bottom of it. I know B.C. was in there *somewhere.*

Malone wanted a new car. I knew that, so the only thing I did to help him out was set him up with a car dealer who was a friend or a relative of Uncle Charlie. I never handed over any money for that red and white Grand Prix—or was it red and black? Anyway, Moses eventually settled for a Chrysler Imperial arranged for by Maryland.

Other than the rumors, life was pretty boring in Petersburg. It rained a good deal and we wore out a deck of cards playing gin rummy in our hotel room. Sometimes we would go out for a drive or do some shopping but mostly Harrison and I took turns. We wanted to have someone by the telephone in case something broke...and we were expecting something to bust open any minute.

In order to keep Malone thinking about Clemson, we even got Tree Rollins involved. Both Tree and Skip Wise telephoned Mo, giving him the soft sell. Moses was interested in playing forward at Clemson; most of the other schools wanted him as a center. We already had our center in Rollins and Moses liked the idea of playing next to Tree. Plus, he liked Tree as a person. Those were his reasons for wanting Clemson. As Harrison told me,

"I don't think Moses is interested in going to school. He just wants to come to a school to play basketball, not get an education." I agreed with Charlie. Mo only wanted a school to work on his moves before moving on to the professional ranks.

Each school was using various methods to catch Malone. New Mexico, for example, used the team manager of Mo's high school team as a contact. The manager was a tiny fellow and whenever Whisenant wanted to deliver a message he'd summon this kid. New Mexico was running all sorts of notes into the Malone house almost every day.

Maryland was also employing some last minute strategy. Howard White, in particular, was doing a lot of errand running. He was what I called the go-for...go for this and go for that. White would drive back to College Park, Maryland about two hours away and pick up some girls on campus to bring back to Petersburg.

I don't think Lefty Driesell really knew some of the stuff which was going on, especially what Howard White was doing. Look, a lot of head coaches don't know *everything* their assistants do. Some don't want to know. Besides, these assistants are under a helluva lot of pressure when they're recruiting. If they don't produce often enough, they're soon gone.

Assistants generally are a nervous breed, too. I mean, I heard the story about one assistant coach in the ACC who, while driving the head coach's rental car in North Carolina, drove it through a mud puddle, splashing mud all over the hubcaps. Well, later that night that assistant was seen with a towel, down on his hands and knees, wiping off the mud. It was in the middle of the night and he was wearing a three piece suit. Talk about paranoia!

Lefty's top assistant, Dave Pritchett, was a particularly nervous sort. But he was a hustler. A day never had enough hours for Dave when it came to recruiting. He would go to great lengths to recruit a ballplayer.

Which brings to mind The Great Chase we had with Pritchett through the streets of Petersburg during our recruitment of Moses Malone.

Remember, we had lost contact with Malone after he disappeared from his hotel room. Maryland, however, didn't know that. Lefty and his gang still believed we knew where Moses was hiding out.

This one particular evening Harrison went out to get some sandwiches and a six pack of beer. While he was driving, Charlie noticed someone was following his car. He drove to a 7-11 and the car was still behind him. He got out of the car and noticed the person in the car behind him watching him. So Charlie drove around several more blocks to make sure. He stopped in for another six-pack. The car was still tailing him. Finally, Charlie got back to the Holiday Inn and told me the story. Time was passing pretty slowly so I suggested we go out and have some fun.

We decided to take a ride...a long ride. About four hours.

We drove to just about every possible street in Petersburg, stopping only for a beer or to hit the bathroom. We took turns at the wheel. I bet Pritchett was bleary-eyed from tailing us, but you've got to give him credit, he never lost sight of our car. He stayed right with us. I couldn't believe it.

Talk about dedication beyond the call of duty...

On the other hand I guess I could understand how Pritchett felt. Everybody was paranoid about the next fellow making a move, THE MOVE which might capture Moses Malone. I was paranoid, too. I felt *everyone* was following me. I thought the NCAA was following us; I thought the media was on our tail. I was paranoid. I drank a lot of beer and was popping diet pills to quiet my fears. I was a nervous wreck.

Then it all came to a halt.

At 7:15 a.m. on June 20, Malone finally announced his decision. Maryland was the lucky school, which I'm sure made Mary Malone very happy. According to a story from an eyewitness to the signing, Robertnett Hayes walked into Moses' bedroom that morning with Maryland's letter-of-intent and asked Mo if he would like to sign. Mo supposedly got this big smile on his face, mumbled "yes", signed the document and then rolled over and went back to sleep. Downstairs it was said Lefty blurted out, "Moses, you've made me the happiest man in the world."

Well, Mo didn't make me too happy, but I was relieved. It was over. When we checked out of the Holiday Inn the man handed us a bill for $183.26.

During those 11 days in Petersburg, I can't tell you how much I felt like a fool. I remember Harrison telling me, "Tates, this thing stunk. I'm makin' up my mind I'm never gonna do it again. If this is what it takes to win the national championship, I don't want it. This is not what basketball is all about. Or recruiting."

I couldn't agree more. If I had to do it all over again myself I would have left Petersburg the first day. But I had been told to stay put, so like a good obedient servant I stayed.

I had been nothing more than a puppet for B.C. Inabinet. With all the alleged money that was being offered to Malone—and again I want to make it clear I didn't know the specifics—I was made to feel like a slave buyer. If anyone ever tries to do that to me again I'll tell them to fuck themselves.

I wound up losing all self-respect for myself, not only because of the way we tried to get Malone, but more importantly for allowing myself to be placed under B. C.'s foot. I remember a year later, after my dismissal from Clemson, B.C. wrote me a note. It said, "Now you're gonna know who your friends really are." I wrote him a note back. "My friends have already called me."

It wasn't until I got B. C. Inabinet completely off my back that I started to feel good about myself again. Unfortunately, I had not known of any other way *but* to go along with him. I mean, B. C. had all this money. He had the balls to do these kinds of things and the ability to sell. He knew how to wrap people around his finger, including me.

In fact, I'm sure he still has people bowing to him. B. C. remains very active with Clemson's athletic program and still gives them a lot of money. I'll say this, he is very loyal to his alma mater. A guy like that, however, makes me think. I wonder how many people like him are out there at other schools?

Personally, I feel there are plenty. This kind of cheating is going on right now at schools all over our country. There are prominent members of a university's alumni, people with big bucks, who annually pick up mortgage payments on an athlete's home, buy him cars or clothing, provide him and his family with insurance programs or real estate deals. All those things can be done so easily without the public knowing. It's so easy to circumvent the rules. All an alumnus has to do is donate his money and keep his mouth shut.

It's only when an alumnus' ego or mouth gets in the way that the trouble starts. There are some guys who have to let everyone know that they bought a particular player. That's how the word gets out, which leads to an NCAA investigation.

It happened that way at Clemson.

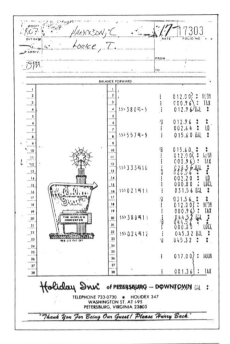

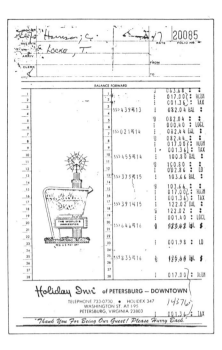

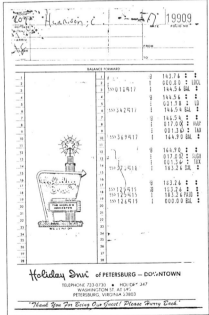

I spent 11 days in Petersburg in an attempt to persuade Moses Malone to come to Clemson. This bill from the Holiday Inn is all I came away with.

In Search of Moses

Malone's Uncle Denies Offers From Clemson

By CHARLES PASCHAL
Record Sports Writer

The uncle of high school basketball star Moses Malone today denied any under-the-table offers as inducement to recruit the highly-sought cager.

Several newspapers quoted Charlie Hudgins, the uncle of the 6-11 Petersburg, Va. star who will be attending Maryland, as saying he had offers of $1,000 twice from Clemson to help secure an automobile for the player.

In a telephone conversation with The Columbia Record today, Hudgins said:

"I want to clear this thing up. I have received no offers from anyone. I've heard reports that I got offers from Clemson, New Mexico and Oral Roberts, but none of it is true."

Hudgins' denial is in direct conflict with what Hudgins reportedly told United Press International reporter Steve Calford when the story broke six days ago.

"I haven't told anyone that," said Hudgins. "All that came from Moses' mother, Mary. I don't know why she would do it. I'm going on television tonight to try and clean it up."

Hudgins said more may break in the story.

"I don't think everything's known," he said. "Moses did not want to go to Maryland, but Lefty Driesell (Maryland coach) got close to her, and there was just no changing her mind. She was helped to get a better job, which may have made up her mind."

Clemson Coach Tates Locke flatly denied making any illegal overtures to Malone or his relatives and said he hoped the NCAA would investigate the charges.

"There was never any kind of inducement to that young man," Locke declared. "It is really ridiculous. "I can't believe they would say that."

Mrs. Malone also has charged that the University of New Mexico recruiter let her son use his rented car while the recruiter camped near the Malone home.

Although Maryland has signed the star, the NCAA and the Atlantic Coast Conference are investigating the charges of illegal recruiting.

"I haven't even been in town," Hudgins said. "I've been in New York and at Virginia Beach. I get back and read all this. Mary gave them the quotes, because I haven't been in town.

"Hudgins said he was upset "because I became real good friends with Coach Locke. That's why I'm going on television, to let the public know what is going on in this mess."

Malone was the subject of a bitter recruiting war for his talents, which are good enough for a professional offer, the first ever extended to a prep star. The Utah Stars drafted the youngster out of high school.

APPEARED IN THE COLUMBIA RECORD ON JULY 8, 1974.

10
RUNNING SCARED

Losing the battle—or maybe I should call it the war—to sign Moses Malone was indeed a setback for us but it proved to be only the beginning of a miserable summer in 1974.

The pressure and public criticism was coming from all directions. There was some preliminary talk of an NCAA investigation and that worried me. Then there was trouble even in our own backyard. Right there in Clemson. I think some of the alums didn't like the idea of us having so many blacks on our ballclub—we would have six in 1974-75. They said we had "too many niggers for our own good." My assistants began to feel the heat, especially Charlie Harrison.

I remember the day Charlie called me up. He was distraught.

"Tates, a guy just called my house and said, 'If you recruit any more of them niggers you're not gonna be safe in the streets.' "

I told Charlie to sit tight.

Other telephone calls followed. People would call and make brief threats or just hang up. I'll tell you, it was making me a nervous wreck, as if I needed something *else* to make me nervous. I was still popping a lot of diet pills and drinking heavily. Beer or scotch and milk.

I was a different person. Charlie Harrison recognized that.

"His whole personality took a turn, that's for sure," agreed Harrison. "Whether it was a result of those pills or the booze I don't know, but I do know Tates was super hyper that summer. Looking back, I think it was this anxiety which caused him to make some bad decisions which poisoned his personal life. I think it contributed to his bad judgement...he was reaching for something to kind of soothe him. I know he didn't agree with the things that had gone on in our recruitment of Moses Malone. He knew we had gone a bit too far in recruiting him.

"I was only 22 at the time, a bit naive myself, but I really liked coach Locke. I had met Tates at Bobby Knight's basketball camp the summer before (1973). I had been a graduate assistant for Bobby at Indiana University and this one day Knight asked me to pick Tates up at the airport. He was flying in to give a clinic to the kids. Well, that began our friendship.

"Tates has a lot of trust in people. I know he comes across as being dumb to some folks, but that's because he's been kicked around so much. Really, the guy is super sharp. Then too, another reason I've gotten along with Tates so well is that he understands me...he never pitied me or said things behind my back.

"I contracted polio at birth and have always walked with a limp. Hey, the doctors told me when I was a kid that I'd never walk, but I even managed to make my varsity basketball team in my senior year at high school in Scotland Neck, North Carolina, a small town near Rocky Mount. Only averaged a point a game as a substitute but I made the team.

"Basketball has always been a big part of my life, just as it has been for Tates. In fourth grade I was the team manager for the varsity and later, between the sixth and twelfth grades, I was the team athletic trainer.

"I'm a competitor, so I can relate to Tates' personality. I also know Tates must have taken some flack for hiring me. There are a lot of coaches at other NCAA schools who say things about me because of my bad leg —that's been obvious to me. Things such as, 'How can you hire *that* guy?' or 'How could Tates recruit a cripple for a coach, a guy who's never played the game?'

"Some people feel Tates hired me out of sympathy...people in this profession can be so cruel. That's where Tates was so different. He never once lied to me. Oh, sometimes he wouldn't tell me some things to protect me, but he never lied to me.

"I remember after I came on board in the fall of 1973, about a week later assistant coach George Hill resigned. Even later, another assistant, Cliff Malpass, wrote a letter trying to get Tates fired. That was prior to the 1974-75 season. So Tates had to get rid of Malpass. Through all this internal trouble Tates confided in me. Like I said, I was a young kid and sometimes the things which were going on made me uncomfortable...I wasn't really ready for all of this. Not yet.

"It (the cheating) was something I couldn't live with and I think Tates realized this. He knew I didn't like being involved... I mean, coaching basketball is tough enough but it's certainly no fun when somebody's riding over you with a damn hammer.

"That's the way Tates felt that summer and all through the following season. He was losing control over what he loved—coaching basketball. Working with young men. He was left minding the store and hoping things would go right. What he wasn't doing was coaching basketball.

"He was dyin' inside. I told him, 'Tates, there's no way you're gonna be able to survive all this. There's too much controversy.' Everywhere we went, in Clemson or on the road, there was controversy following us.

"In some respects it was intriguing because there was so much coming down. It was unbelievable. It seemed to me that Tates, somewhere or somehow, had pissed off the wrong people. I don't know whether it was his personality or his personal life or maybe the way he handled the players, but I felt there were people out there who wanted to get him, one way or another.

"I felt everywhere we went, people were lookin' at us as criminals. You'd have thought Tates and I had gone out and killed somebody.''

Believe me, I knew exactly what Charlie meant.

Actually, we knew there would be a good chance the NCAA would investigate Clemson's basketball program long before the summer of 1974. Really, the probe probably was launched about the time we signed Tree Rollins in the spring of '73. At the time, the NCAA was investigating Auburn's athletic program and since they had also tried to recruit Rollins, I'm sure a lot of that investigation led to us. I'm sure it was the recruitment of Rollins which started the ball rolling.

There were other contributing factors, however. I'm convinced one of our own players, Ricky Hunt, turned us into the NCAA.

Hunt was a kid we had recruited from De Matha High School in suburban Washington, D. C., a big fellow at 6-6 and 230 pounds. Ricky, though, had a bunch of personal problems and one of them was not keeping his weight down. In his first season, he turned in a good job for the freshman team, finishing third in scoring with a 15.1 average and second to Wayne Croft in rebounding at 9.4. Then he got heavy and the added bulk cut into his effectiveness the following season, his first and only campaign on the varsity.

I got down on Ricky and told him to lose some weight, that I wasn't going to play him unless he complied. He took offense to my directive and to the fact we were beginning to open our pocketbooks to some of the incoming recruits, people like Tree and Jo Jo.

It was while discussing the NCAA investigation with Kentucky assistant coach Lynn Nance, who previously worked for the NCAA and was part of the team sent into investigate Clemson, that I learned a member of our team had spilled his guts to the NCAA. Nance never told me it was Ricky Hunt, but by piecing together some of the facts he offered, I *knew* it was Hunt. I knew it was him because one of the NCAA accusations involved Clemson buying a pair of work boots for a ballplayer so he could work his construction job in the summer. I remember buying Hunt a pair of boots for just that reason...and no one outside of myself, Ricky and maybe his parents knew about those boots.

So it had to have been Hunt who contacted Nance.

It had also been mentioned to Nance that Tree had received a new car, that Jo Jo had a used car and that I gave permission to certain players to use my speed boat for water skiing and my pontoon boat for partying on Lake Hartwell, which adjoins the Clemson campus with about 100 miles of shoreline.

It's true I lent some of the kids the boats, but these boats were available for use by *any* of my friends who called and asked me to let them use them. The privilege was open for anyone who was a member of the Clemson student body. In fact my wife was an officer for a sorority on campus—Kappa Alpha Theta—and she let them use the boats on numerous occasions. The Clemson cheerleaders also used them.

Anyway, Ricky was a vindictive kid at the time but I can't place the finger on him for being the sole reason behind the investigation. I can't say he was the main cause. *I* was the main cause. Once you open Pandora's Box and get into giving players illegal inducements you can't ever stop. You can't take gifts away from players once they've already been handed out. Once you start making it a practice, you have to continue.

My mistake was not walking away from Clemson after my first year, for not being smart enough to see that the cheating could have somehow been avoided. But I wasn't smart.

In the fall of '74, I went to Lexington, Kentucky to visit Nance to try and find out more about the investigation. That's when I learned some of the things which put me onto Ricky Hunt. My intention for visiting Nance was to find out what information the NCAA had on us...how much investigating had actually been done. I asked Nance what I should do. Should I stick it out or should I resign? That's all I wanted to know.

All Nance could tell me was 'You're in over your head'. He wouldn't tell me anything else. He said he couldn't.

I returned to campus and decided to fight the criticism, which by now was being heard almost daily by myself and my staff. I was stupid for continuing; I was fighting a losing battle. If I had it to do over again, I would have gotten myself a very, very good lawyer and fought it or resigned. I didn't do either.

Like a fool, I leaned on B.C. Inabinet, school president R. C. Edwards and other members of the Clemson administration for advice. They kept on telling me, "We're gonna back you to the end"...those were their exact words. I didn't know it at the time, but in reality they were setting me up to be the sacrificial lamb.

I guess it was Tree Rollins' mother who first tipped me off the end was near, that B. C. was already lobbying for my dismissal. Wilma Robinson had come up for a game in January and we had a conversation afterward.

"Tates, B. C. doesn't like the way you're running the team," was the message from Wilma. "I hear he's gonna see to it that you're not around next season. That's the truth."

Wilma was upset, so upset that she told me she was making plans to have Tree transfer to another school. She didn't want Tree at Clemson without me as his coach.

That conversation took place in January of 1975, around the time we began a winning streak which would raise our record from 6-7 to 17-9. But the winning apparently didn't change B. C.'s feelings. I believe he was still pissed off at me for telling him to keep his big mouth shut at the ACC tournament in March of 1974, when he blurted out, "I bought Tree Rollins and Tates can't win with him."

I told him it was a stupid statement to make publicly, that it would get back to the wrong people. He reportedly made other statements, very similar in nature, at other social gatherings. It was getting worse and worse, but of course he denied his involvement. But at least twice a month someone called my office to tell me B. C. was running off at the mouth.

While we were having problems off the court, we also had our share of problems on the court...at least in the beginning of the season.

We had a very talented team and our players knew it. A good many of them regarded themselves as stars—they were on ego trips. It was very difficult to get them to play together, right from the very outset of fall practice which began October 15.

Skip Wise was a pain in the butt in the beginning. I had to discipline him a couple of times and even benched him early that season. He'd be late for practice continuously and sometimes would dog it during workouts. Maybe it was the fact I was the first white coach he had ever played for, but all I know is that it was a difficult adjustment for the kid.

We won three of our first four games and lost six of the next nine. It was during this period that Wayne Croft, Jo Jo Bethea and Tree Rollins became our team leaders. I think they took over out of fear—I really do. I guess they thought I might kick their butts if we kept on losing. I know *something* got to Tree, who normally doesn't say 'boo' to anybody. After we lost by 15 points to Louisville December 18, Tree came into the locker room and verbally undressed his teammates. He was hot. That was the same game I had punished Wise, who had scored 86 points in our first four games, for missing practice before the trip. Skip never got off the bench against Louisville.

Then we went to Dayton, Ohio for the Dayton Invitational, December 20-21. This is my wife Nancy's hometown, where her parents, the Craigs, live. We were the best team in that four-team field but we got beat twice, by La Salle and Dayton. We were humiliated. I was pissed...couldn't care less if Christmas was a few days away. In fact, I was so mad that after Charlie

Harrison and the squad flew back to Clemson, I called Charlie on the phone and told him to fly back to Dayton with *every* film of *every* game we had played the past two seasons.

We sat up all night, till daybreak, looking at those films and drinking Bristol Creme. I really got wasted that night.

Next we visited Minneapolis for the Pillsbury Classic, December 27-28. We couldn't get the court for practice until 1 a.m., so we worked the kids until three, then practiced two more times later that day. We really crammed our entire offense into their heads. We went back to the basics, forgetting the free-and-easy passes and that kind of bullshit. I made them run plays and I put Jo Jo in charge. Then we opened up the inside for Tree and let Croft do more passing. Wayne passed the ball so much he finished leading the ACC in assists.

At last we had the team playing to its strengths and I was in complete charge of the show. Soon, our fortunes changed. We split the two games in the Christmas tourney, then tuned up for the ACC season with an easy win over Southern Florida.

When we returned to Clemson January 5 to open against Virginia we were 5-5, but inside I felt we were getting ready to bust things wide open. I arrived several hours before our afternoon game with the Cavaliers and was going over some game plans in the locker room when Charlie Harrison walked in. He had this peculiar look on his face.

"Coach, there's a welcoming party for you outside," Charlie told me.

Sure enough, there was. People had brought signs and posters and placed them all around Littlejohn Coliseum. Signs which said, "Terminate Tates", "Goodbye Locke" or "Get The Players To Fire The Coach". It was more like a lynching party.

So much for the home court advantage that game. Oh well, we went out and beat Virginia, then headed to Tobacco Road for games against North Carolina and Duke. It was about this time the newspapers started firing bullets. Now we were being hit from all sides.

We arrived in Chapel Hill and were greeted by headlines which told of how we had given players airplane tickets, clothing and cars. A week later it was repeated in Durham. Some of the rumors, of course, were true, but there were some which were way off base. A couple were tasteless or distracting, like the article in Chapel Hill which said Skip Wise and I weren't communicating and that Skip was planning to transfer after the season. What hogwash.

That one made my blood boil.

We got beat in Carolina by two points after going only 17-for-29 from the foul line. Naturally, I was upset. I was really hot and it had nothing to do with the fact the temperature inside Carolina's hot gym made the place feel like a sauna. I was more steamed over the clips concerning Skip and myself.

After the game I pulled out the clip from the newspaper and challenged anyone from that paper at the post-game interview session. One reporter moved forward and I got in his face.

"Get your ass outta here," I screamed at him. "I don't have to talk to you or anyone else."

And I didn't.

But this was only the beginning. It got worse in late January and February on the road. There was no way to stop it.

I wasn't the only person who questioned whether Clemson was being sabotaged in the press. An editor of a national publication, Larry Donald of *Basketball Weekly,* flew into the Carolinas to do a story on us and he asked me what was going on. He couldn't believe it either. We were convicted long before the NCAA made its official decision.

The stands were just full of hatred everywhere we played. The fans would yell, "How much money you got tied up in that guy?" or "Who's got the best car?" or "Tates, you look like a thief." It was brutal, but somehow I kept my temper under control. I was tempted to go after some fans physically but I never did. I had to set an example for my players. I told them to close their ears and bite the bullet, to try and use the negative publicity as an incentive to win. "They can't stop us from winning games," I told them frequently.

I think a lot of the players were more concerned about my welfare than their own. Tree was very concerned.

So were my parents, who lived only a few miles away from Clemson in Easley, South Carolina. All these reports of a cheating scandal in the newspapers were very embarrassing to them. I was their only child, so I knew they were hurt. But they disguised their feelings well. Mom and dad are very humble people. Dad had worked hard all his life as a manufacturer's representative, one of those guys who peddled things door-to-door. In a small community I'm sure the negative publicity hurt him deeply.

Both of them kept asking me if I had done anything wrong. My dad probably understood the situation best. He knew I was a competitive person, someone who didn't like to lose. I never revealed the details of how we got our prospects to campus, how we kept them there, but I really think dad had it all figured out.

I kept telling my parents things would turn out okay, that the administration promised to stand behind me 100 percent. I got the impression they were satisfied with that explanation, but looking back to some conversations I had with them after I got fired I know my folks were hiding their feelings. Dad was especially miffed at the school for hanging me out to dry. He knew Clemson was setting me up, using me as the fall guy.

I believe he tried to explain to my mom what happened at Clemson goes on all over the country at other schools; that what I had done was nothing in violation of the United States Constitution. I did not steal, I did not deface and I did not kill or beat anybody up. All I had done, he told mom, was go about my job the way the school wanted me to in order to perform my duties. Maybe it wasn't the *right* way, but the school was the employer and their son was only the employee.

Poor mom. I believe she thought my crimes were as bad as robbing a bank or embezzlement. She thought if it wasn't so big a deal, why was the media putting me in the headlines daily?

There were also internal problems on the squad. The white players were upset over the money paid out to the blacks. There was always a fight in practice and I think some of it was because of this animosity.

Others complained about the way I handled certain players like Skip, Stan Rome, Colon Abraham and Tree. The black players. They thought I had double standards.

There was another problem concerning how I dealt with a player who was reportedly homosexual. A couple of players didn't like the way I handled that issue.

The main problem, the one which caused a big split, concerned a letter which had supposedly been written by a player. In it he criticized me for the way I handled the black players and disclosed some of the "favors" the star players were receiving. This anonymous player reportedly handed over the letter to our team physician who, in turn, refused to reveal the contents or the author. He told me he couldn't do it "because it would break a medical trust."

That set off a wild witch hunt by me and my staff. By now we realized we had a real sicko on our team, a sicko who was trying to split the club down the middle. He was going to ruin the season and attract more attention by the NCAA.

We had to find out his identity.

We never did.

To this day I can't say for sure the letter really existed, but I know there had to be some truth to it. Surely, we had enough meetings over it so that it *seemed* real to us. Finally, out of desperation, I approached the doctor hoping to work out a deal.

"You tell whoever it is that I'll resign if he will tear that letter up," I told the doctor. "Tell him the team and school are a helluva lot more important than me."

The mysterious letter surfaced in the fall and followed me around for much of the season. I guess after that I had an inkling that I might be on my way out. When Tree's mother told me B. C.'s comments in January I *knew* I was finished.

It became a matter of *when* the ax would fall.

I didn't know where to turn. I felt terrible about my professional life; I felt miserable about my personal life. I didn't know what to expect or where I was going. I had no idea about my future. All I know is that I felt guilty and miserable. I felt like I wanted to run and hide. I couldn't hide but I did run. I stopped popping pills, cut out the booze and took up long distance running. I'd run about eight or nine miles a day.

Running is the only way I kept my sanity.

TIGS INK A-A WISE • CLEMSON UNIVERSITY HEAD BASKETBALL COACH TATES LOCKE SIGNED HIS SECOND ALL-AMERICA BASKETBALL PLAYER IN AS MANY DAYS SATURDAY WHEN SKIP WISE OF DUNBAR HIGH SCHOOL IN BALTIMORE, MD., INKED A GRANT-IN-AID WITH THE TIGERS.
"I HAVE NEVER BEEN AROUND A MORE POLISHED BASKETBALL PLAYER AT THIS POINT IN HIS CAREER," LOCKE SAID AFTER SIGNING WISE."

Skip Wise

GUARD • COLON ABRAHAM
6'6"

GUARD - SKIP WISE • 6'4"
HIGH SCHOOL ALL-AMERICA
1ST TEAM PARADE
PRO • PROSPECT
PRE-LAW PLANNED

CLEMSON'S
1974-1976
DREAM TEAM

ALL-AMERICA 3RD TEAM
COACH AND ATHLETE
PRO • PROSPECT
GUARD
GUIDANCE STUDIES

The News and Observer, Sunday Jan 6, 1974, II—3
Terrapins' Elmore:
Rollins Woke Me Up

ACC CHAMPS?
1974-1977

NCAA CHAMPS?
1974-1977

WAYNE "TREE" ROLLINS • 7'1"
ALL ACC - 1974?
PRO • PROSPECT!
RECREATION & PUBLIC RELATIONS

DRIESELL, AT
COLUMBIA STATE,
PRAISES
ROLLINS 1.6.74

ROLLINS: NOT JUST ANOTHER BIG MAN!

ROME HONORED AS TOP ATHLETE

VERSATILE STAN ROME, WHO HAS SIGNED A BASKETBALL GRANT WITH TATES LOCKE'S CLEMSON TIGERS, HAS BEEN NAMED AS THE NATION'S TOP HIGH SCHOOL ATHLETE BY PARADE MAGAZINE, A PUBLICATION THAT ALSO TABBED THE VALDOSTA, GA. NATIVE ON ITS PREP ALL-AMERICAN CAGE UNIT.
ROME, APPARENTLY CONVINCED OF THE FUTURE OF CLEMSON'S WAYNE "TREE" ROLLINS, THEN DECIDED ON THE ATLANTIC COAST CONFERENCE SCHOOL OVER OTHER OFFERS.

STAN ROME

FORWARD - STAN ROME
HIGH SCHOOL ALL-AMERICA
1ST TEAM PARADE
PRO - PROSPECT!
BASKETBALL & FOOTBALL
OLYMPIC TRACK POTENTIAL
• BUSINESS STUDY

THE MISSING LINK
AND
• THE ONLY 1 MO

"D FULFILL
A DREAM
A FUTURE STAR

MOSES MALONE

FORWARD - "MO" MALONE 6'11"
18 YEAR-OLD INTIMIDATOR

HIGH SCHOOL ALL-AMERICA 1S
PARADE 1ST. TEAM

PRO - DRAFTEE!
EDUCATION WANTED

Clemson crowd goes "bananas" during the 1974-75 season.

Stan Rome is on the floor in a 1974-75 game against the University of Maryland. Skip Wise (10) and Tree Rollins (30) look on. That's John Lucas (15) of Maryland and Steve Sheppard (10) of Maryland.

Tree Rollins is introduced on TV before an ACC game.

Tree Rollins pictured with his mother, Wilma Robinson.

Tree Rollins deplanes after a victory.

Skip Wise, Clemson player.

Ricky Hunt, Clemson player.

Colon Abraham, Clemson player.

Moses Malone, the recruit that got away.

Jo Jo Bethea takes a jump shot from the corner against The Citadel.

Phil Ford, former Clemson great, in action against The Denver Nuggets.

Skip Wise (10) takes a breather on the court during a game against Furman in the 1974-75 season. The search is on for a lost contact lens.

Tates Locke prowls the sidelines .

11
DISOWNED AND
DISHONORED

The season passed slowly, even though we won nine of 10 games during one stretch between January 18 and February 22. We finished the 1974-75 season with a 16-9 record and went on to win our first round game against Duke in the ACC tournament. Now we're in the semifinals against North Carolina.

We should have won that game, too, but we missed two shots at the end of regulation play, one by Skip and another by Tree. Carolina came back and beat us in overtime, 76-71. Regardless, we received a bid to the National Invitation Tournament in New York City, the school's first post-season game in its history.

So we went to play in Madison Square Garden and hundreds of important people from Clemson accompanied us for our first-round game against Providence College. All the camp followers were there, including school president Robert C. Edwards, athletic director Bill McLellan and former athletic director Frank Howard. The whole nine yards...anybody who was anybody in the Clemson athletic family.

The alumni was fired up for a big social gathering in New York when our team arrived but I knew we still had to play a ballgame so I tried to keep the situation under control. I didn't want the kids to run off into the East River.

R.C. Edwards was never more friendly to me than he was that weekend. In fact, both he and his wife kept a close watch on my sons, John and Mike, whom I had brought along for the games. Like I said, Edwards was bending over backwards to be nice so I started to think that maybe all the rumors about my imminent demise were wrong. Maybe my self guilt had gotten the best of me.

Maybe I wasn't going to have my head chopped off.

On the day of the game, which we would lose by five points, I intercepted a $250 moneygram sent to Skip Wise. It had come compliments of a member of the Clemson alumni. I didn't give it to Skip, instead keeping it with the intention of bringing it to the attention of Edwards and McLellan when we returned to Clemson.

It had reached a point where I had to draw the line.

I told Charlie Harrison, "I just can't live with myself doing these things anymore. I gotta call a meeting."

Charlie replied: "You ought to go in there and tell them you can't coach these guys like this anymore, that you're a coach, a teacher, and you can't do those things while all that other crap is going on."

So I telephoned Edwards and arranged for an interview Monday morning, March 17.

On the way back home I got to thinking about my relationship with Frank Howard and his career at Clemson. Frank and I were fairly close, I guess because I was his last official act as athletic director in 1970-71. He was always very open and blunt with me when we talked, which we did quite often in the little office the school let him maintain in the athletic complex.

It was rather sad what Edwards and his gang had done to Howard. Here was a man who had put the school on the map with his excellent football teams, who had shown the school how to make money in athletics. What's more, it was Frank Howard who got the school involved in outside money-making ventures. He got them to own their own book store; it was Frank who originated IPTAY. He did all these things only to have Edwards push him out the door.

How ironic. After all, it was Howard who had given R.C. his first job at Clemson—as football team manager. How quickly he forgot. Now, years later with a chance to reciprocate, Edwards bit Howard in the ass. It was really a shame.

That should have told me something about Clemson; in fact, Howard himself had tried to tell me a few things about the school that year, particularly about Edwards. We'd be sitting in his office and Howard would say, "Tates, you're in a lot of trouble here and you're gonna be the dispensable one in this whole thing."

It's too bad Frank did not remain athletic director. I think if he had stayed most of what occurred at Clemson might not have happened. At least not to the same extent. I honestly believe Frank would not have put the same amount of pressure on me or my basketball program which Bill McLellan did. And I don't think Howard would have panicked. As Charlie Harrison told me, "A lot of people ran scared in the end, putting the blame in other places."

McLellan was one of these people. So was Edwards.

I was thinking about some of these things while mentally preparing for my meeting that Monday. I had a list of things I wanted to get off my chest. I wanted to find out about the renewal of my contract and what plans the administration had for fighting the NCAA investigation. I also wanted to show Edwards and McLellan the moneygram sent to Wise and ask them to put some cuffs on the heavy-handed members of the alumni.

The meeting that Monday took place in Walter Cox's office. Cox was the vice president for student affairs. When I arrived I saw Cox and McLellan but I couldn't believe Edwards was not there. I was told he couldn't attend, that he had been called out of town, but later I found out he *was* at school but didn't *want* to attend.

Instead he sent McLellan and Cox to do his dirty work.

Believe me, it was dirty. Before I got a word out of my mouth both men were throwing shit in my face. They told me I had not been a good member of the Clemson family. It was a favorite phrase, "the Clemson family", one which they had thrown in my face before.

Since my arrival at Clemson I think both McLellan and Cox had regarded me as somewhat of a rogue, someone who was always at odds with the school's football program and whose personal conduct was unbecoming of a Clemson athletic official.

They started in with this same criticism before I managed to get a word in edgewise.

"Are you telling me," I asked, "that I'm no longer going to be working at Clemson?"

"No, no," they returned. "You can stay on here but we just don't want you to be the basketball coach any longer. With the NCAA investigation coming to a head we feel it would be best for you to sit back and keep a low profile. We'd like for you to resign."

Resign? The word stung my pride. I told them it was out of the question.

"First of all," I explained, "by me resigning I'm going to be admitting my guilt. I don't think it's in the best interests of the university to do this. Furthermore, and more importantly, it's not in my own best interest."

They shook their heads and insisted the decision was final.

Now it got real emotional.

"I really don't give a goddam about the university anymore," I shouted, my voice filled with emotion. "I'm thinking about myself for a change. For five years I've thought about this university. Everything I've done has been for this institution."

I listed some of my sacrifices, particularly going along with B.C. Inabinet's schemes. I said to them, "Who instructed me to fly to Rocky Mount in B.C.'s plane and get Phil Ford's parents to sign a phony affadavit? It was you, Bill. Now you expect me to sit here and take all this crap?"

McLellan said, "You're just emotional now."

"You're goddam right I'm emotional," I shot back. "This is my livelihood." Then I turned to Cox. "You say I'm not a member of the Clemson family? Well, who was the *only* guy from this department who helped your son out the night he drove his speed boat into a stone pillar at the bridge? I was the first guy there, worried about *your* son. Where do you get off tellin' me I'm not a member of the Clemson family?"

I went on and listed my accomplishments in my five seasons. I mentioned how our program had improved, how we had gone to a post-season tournament for the first time in the school's history. How we had gotten national recognition in the polls. How attendance at the Coliseum had skyrocketed. Those kinds of things. Then I brought up the ticket drives and other promotions launched under my direction. I went through everything.

It became a war in that room and I got hysterical. I started to cry. Then I got mad. It was all I could do to keep from reaching across the table and grabbing their fat asses. I stormed out of the office with both Cox and McLellan in pursuit, yelling for me to come back. I guess they were afraid I was going to blab to the newspapers. As I passed Cox's secretary I gave her a message as well. "You're as bad as those fat guys in that room," I told her, "because you all gossip like a bunch of old people."

I ran down the steps and out the building, hopped into my car and drove off. I just drove and drove and drove. I only stopped to contact my two assistant coaches. I got hold of Bill Clendinen and I reached Charlie Harrison in New York, where he was recruiting. Then I drove to the golf course in Greenville.

Back at school, McLellan and Cox sent out search parties. They finally caught up with me at the 13th hole. "We gotta have another meeting," one of them said. "We have to get you to sign some papers."

"I ain't gonna sign shit," I said. "I'm gonna golf today, go fishing tomorrow and then I'm gonna find something else to do."

They kept saying, "You gotta do this" or "You gotta do that."

Three days later I sent McLellan a formal letter of resignation and a few days after that I released another statement to the press. Later that year I would issue ·a short statement summarizing my part in the illegal activities at Clemson. It read:

I am very sorry it happened. During the past several months I have cooperated fully with school and NCAA officials answering honestly all questions and accusations that were put before me.

In a lengthy notarized report to the NCAA, I admitted my guilt and defended my innocence with respect to all specific areas in question. However, the NCAA held me responsible for all the violations.

I feel I carried the burden of guilt for the entire school and its representatives. I know a lot of people will wonder that if I am not guilty then who is? I am going to refrain from dragging this issue out and I don't want to implicate anyone else as I feel there have been enough people hurt already. I just hope that those individuals in question can live with their consciences as I have to do with mine.

I was hired to do a job and dedicated five years of my life, time-wise, family-wise and financially speaking to succeed. In order to succeed I had to do some things of which I am not proud, and did not believe in at the time.

One area of the NCAA investigation has always bothered me. When the NCAA released its detailed list of infractions against the school (see statement at the conclusion of this chapter) most every violation used phrases like "the former head basketball coach gave" or the "former head basketball coach provided". This implied I was aware of or responsible for every infraction. That just isn't true.

Furthermore, when Clemson never challenged the NCAA news release, it was basically admitting I *was* guilty of all the infractions. The school knew I was not aware of many of these violations but instead of making the NCAA aware of these misleading facts, the school officials sold me down the river. They used my name to shield themselves from the blame.

My first few weeks away from Clemson I fished and played golf. There are days during that period that are blanks in my mind...five or six straight days I don't remember one thing about. The situation really did me in. I do remember going to West Point at their request. They wanted my advice about the type of individual they should hire as coach. They also brought Bobby Knight up for a talk. Bobby and I both told them to hire one of their own people.

The trip back to West Point brought back plenty of memories. I spent a couple good years there, two of the best of my coaching career. Both of my teams went to the NIT and finished third. When I returned to West Point, I found myself doing a lot of reflecting.

Where did I go wrong? Well, I made two bad moves. The first was when I left West Point. I was happy there but I decided to go because of Nancy's health. She was going through some difficult times mentally. The second bad decision was leaving Miami of Ohio. I was just too impatient. I wanted the big time, the ACC. I guess another bad move was not going with Jack Ramsay when he got fired as head coach of the Buffalo Braves. Jack went to Portland as the Trailblazers head man and he wanted me to come along as his assistant, just as I had been in Buffalo. But the Braves offered me the head spot and I thought I'd like being the head honcho of an NBA club. What a sad joke that proved to be.

Anyway, they say a man is allowed to make five mistakes in his life, but not three in a row. I had hit into a triple play. All of a sudden I found myself on the outside looking in.

I wondered if anyone would let me back in.

I hung around Lake Hartwell and went fishing with Harrison for almost a solid month. Every day we were out on the lake. I drank a lot of beer, smoked cigars and grew a beard. I wore the same clothes every day. I think it was during that time that I started thinking about writing this book. It dawned on me how many coaches had done the same thing and really didn't care. They lived with it...it rolled off their backs. It didn't mean anything to them—just a way to get the job done.

Every time I did those things I knew I was cheating. I was actually cheating. And if a guy's going to cheat in basketball he's going to cheat in other areas in his life. When does it stop?

The greatest relief of my life was actually leaving Clemson and those kinds of people. My only problem was I didn't know what to do next. I was sitting around not having the faintest idea what I was going to do. Plus, I was embarrassed over what had happened. Running my summer basketball camp in 1975 was probably the hardest thing I ever had to do. We must have had a thousand kids come to the camp that summer. The people treated me great. I'll never forget some of their kind words, some of their letters.

As much as I dreaded working at that summer camp I had to because of my financial situation. The IRS had come in and knocked me out of about $7,000 or $8,000. We made about $12,000 off the camp and I split that with Clendinen.

I had some long talks with Knight that summer. Of all the people who have known me or worked with me, Bobby probably knows me the best. We went through probably the hardest times in either of our coaching careers together at West Point in 1963 and 1964. We both were going through some personal problems at the time outside of basketball and we fought those things together. He didn't drink—he disapproved of me having even a beer. It was like two guys always watching out for each other.

We fought and argued and to this day we don't ever compare notes. We probably don't talk to each other more than five times a year now but we still remain close. We're like brothers. I know if I didn't have any friends on this earth I could still turn to Bobby. And vice versa. I would lay down whatever I was doing and do what had to be done if Bobby called.

Some people say Bobby is the biggest ass in the world. I don't think that's true. Bobby is not hard to get to know if you want to get to know him, but it's when you get to know him that he really punishes you. You just have to take him for what he is.

I ask Bobby for a lot of advice, times when I really need it. I don't always agree with what he tells me, but normally if I do it the way he suggests it ends up being right. He called me a dumb son-of-a-bitch when I didn't leave Clemson the first year, when I knew what was in store. He really got on me bad, but yet later on he was the first guy to help me. He was the first guy who called me. You know, Bobby knows me better than anybody, even

CAMDEN HIGH SCHOOL
LAURENS STREET
CAMDEN, SOUTH CAROLINA 29020

April 15, 1975

Mr. Tates Locke
Clemson University
Clemson, South Carolina

Dear Coach Locke:

Firstly, I would like to thank you for all that you've done
in helping our Basketball Coaches Association materialize.
Coaches, such as you, have been such an integral part of
making the game what it is today. After hearing your talk
Friday night, I swelled with pride in being associated with
the coaching fraternity.

Secondly, I'm sure a man of your capabilities will get the
opportunity you so richly deserve to do again what you do best.
I look forward to the news announcing, any day, where you'll
be next.

Thirdly, I am asking for the honor of working for you in your
next college position. You probably think I'm crazy since
nothing has been released about a new job, but as I said
earlier, I'm confident you'll be coaching again. Money is no
object--the honor of being associated with you and your program
would be payment enough. Basketball has been and will always
be my life. I hope that you will challenge me with this opportunity.

I sincerely look forward to hearing from you.

Yours in Basketball,

Larry S. DiBiase
Head Basketball Coach

jg

MEMBER OF THE SOUTHERN ASSOCIATION OF COLLEGES AND SECONDARY SCHOOLS

Troy H. Cribb & Sons, Inc.

P O BOX 2908 • 407 S. PINE STREET
SPARTANBURG, SOUTH CAROLINA 29302

April 18, 1975

Mr. Tates Locke
Clemson Athletic Association
Clemson, S.C. 29631
(Please forward)

Dear Tates:

As I have told you after each of the last five years, I truly
enjoyed watching your teams in practice, in regular season and
at tournaments. I saw almost all of our home games, and the
tournaments. For all the pleasure of those events, I thank you.

For most of my own life, I was very successful in anything and
everything that I undertook. Then, several years ago, I made
some serious errors in judgement - and I got some bad breaks at
the same time. All at once, I had serious career problems -
complicated with loss of former friends (at least I had thought
them to be friends) and some family problems - not of my own
making - with my children. For the first time in my life, I
began to feel depressed - defeated, of no use to myself or my
family.

Something happened to help me get my attitude in line - and I
became aware of many, many people who recognized my mistakes and
who still believed in my potential as a contributor in my field.

I put behind me self-recriminations, re-adopted my "I know I can
do it" philosophy and started over. I wish I could say that I
no longer feel unkind toward my former business associates. I
tried to put that behind me because I know energy spent in that
direction diverts me from my goal. Most of the time I can do
that. Sometime it still rankles.

Things are better. Best of all is that I know who and what I am,
and I know that the people who count still believe in me.

During my most difficult time, I sublimated my anxiety over my
situation to interest in your programs. I thought about Hunt and
Croft - and why Doug left - and about DiPasquale telling Dicksie
how good her spaghetti was; and I drove to your practice games in
Greenville and Anderson. I thought you might be interested in your
part in my own situation and experience.

SHIPPERS • PEACHES • CAROLINA YAMS • VEGETABLES

Tates Locke   - 2 -   4/18/75

Very few people - only two or three - know as much as I have told
you, and the remarks are for you to use if you need them, as encouragement from one who believes that, in the right situation and with the
benefit of the pressure-cooker ACC experience, Tates Locke has a great
contribution to make in his field.

I can't think how I might be of help to you - but if _you_ know, please
call on me.

In the meantime, please know that I care about you and your family,
and that I look forward to enjoying the continuance of your great
career.

Please share my letter with your lovely wife, and take for both of
you my very best wishes.

Sincerely yours

Kenneth Cribb

though I don't profess to know him. That would only ruin our relationship, I think.

I enjoy different types of people. I think that is the part I like best about my lifestyle, about my business. I set down certain rules. For instance, if I'm out on business, either coaching or recruiting, we talk about basketball. But if you come into my house we talk about what *you* want to talk about.

When I don't want to be around people I just leave. Maybe it's rude, but I get the hell out. I'm not big on those social functions after ballgames. It's not my kind of thing. When I'm around people I want to laugh. If I'm not laughing I want to go home.

I take great pride in making people laugh. When I got my lunch handed to me at Clemson I made up my mind that never again was I going to be around certain people because I *had* to be around them for fund-raising activities. B.C. Inabinet at Clemson was a good example of this. I felt I *had* to be around him, that it was my duty as basketball coach.

Well, one nice thing about getting canned at Clemson was getting rid of B.C. I didn't think much about that guy the whole time I fished in April and May. I tried to put him completely out of my mind.

Putting Clemson behind me was not easy, especially when Bill Foster was formally announced as the new head coach April 9. I was at Pauley's Island fishing with Harrison when I received the news.

"We were out having a seafood dinner," recalled Harrison. "Tates had a lot to drink and then he gets the phone call that night telling him Foster has been announced as the new head coach. I think the impact, the reality of it, just shattered him.

"That night we slept on the houseboat. All of us were in sleeping bags. I woke up in the middle of the night and there's Tates, standing over me. He reached down with his arms and grabbed my neck. I yelled out, 'Tates, what in the hell are you doin'?' He just rolled over and went back to sleep.

"He must have been having a nightmare. At least I hope it was a nightmare. I hope he wasn't after my ass."

The Complete Text O₁

Below is the complete text of penalties imposed upon Clemson University by the NCAA and a summary of the violations by the university:

Penalty to be Imposed Upon Institution

1. Clemson University shall be publicly reprimanded and censured, and placed on probation for a period of three years, effective September 24, 1975, it being understood that prior to the expiration of this probationary period, the NCAA shall review the University's athletic policies and practices.

2. During the probationary period, Clemson University's intercollegiate basketball team shall end its seasons with the last, regularly scheduled, inseason contest and the University shall not be eligible to participate in the National Collegiate Basketball Championship or any other postseason basketball competition.

3. During the probationary period, Clemson University's intercollegiate basketball team shall not be eligible to appear in any television program subject to the administration and control of this Association, and the institution shall not make any commitments for such appearances during that time.

4. During the 1976-77 academic year, no more than two student-athletes in the sport of basketball shall receive initial, athletically related financial aid (as set forth in O.I. 500) which has been arranged for or awarded by Clemson University.

5. During the 1977-78 academic year, no more than three student-athletes in the sport of basketball shall receive initial, athletically related, financial aid (as set forth in O.I. 500) which has been arranged for or awarded by Clemson University.

6. Clemson University shall be publicly reprimanded for a recruiting violation occurring in the conduct of its intercollegiate football program.

7. In accordance with action taken by Clemson University in response to the "show cause" provision of the NCAA penalty structure, the University's intercollegiate athletic program shall completely sever all relations, whether formal or informal, with certain representatives of the University's athletic interests involved in violations of NCAA legislation in this case including, but not limited to, the representatives financial support, recruiting efforts and membership in institutional booster groups.

Violations of NCAA Legislation

1. NCAA Constitution 3-1-(a)-(3), 3-1-(a)-(6) and 3-1-(a) (amateurism and student participation, extra benefits, and improper financial aid to student-athletes) — The University's former head basketball coach gave a student-athlete cash in excess of face value for the sale of his two Atlantic Coast Conference basketball tournament ticket books.

2. NCAA Constitution 3-1-(a)-(6) and 3-4-(a) (extra benefits and improper financial aid to student-athletes) — (I) On numerous occasions, the University's former head basketball coach and a former assistant basketball coach gave cash in small amounts to certain members of the University's intercollegiate basketball teams to spend for their own personal reasons; (II) The University's former head basketball coach paid a telephone bill charged to a student-athlete at no expense to the young man; (III) The University's former head basketball coach paid, with his own personal funds, charges for work performed on a student-athlete's personal automobile, and (IV) The University's former head basketball coach paid, with his own personal funds, the balance of two bank loans on behalf of a student-athlete.

3. NCAA Constitution 3-1-(e)-(5), 3-1-(g)-(6) and 3-4-(a) (improper expenses, extra benefits and improper financial aid to student-athletes) — (i) Through the arrangements of the University's former head basketball coach, a student-athlete received the benefit of round-trip commercial airline transportation at no charge to the young man between Greenville, South Carolina, and his home; (ii) The University's former head basketball coach gave a student-athlete cash to pay the young man's round-trip commercial airline transportation charges between Greenville, South Carolina, and his home, and (iii) Through the arrangements of the University's former head basketball coach and his personal secretary, a student-athlete received the benefits of round-trip commercial airline transportation between Greenville, South Carolina, and his home at no charge to the young man.

4. NCAA Constitution 3-2 (institutional control) — The involvement of certain representatives of the University's athletic interests in the violations set forth in this case demonstrates that Clemson University did not adequately exercise institutional control and responsibility over these individuals.

5. NCAA Constitution 3-1-(a) and Bylaws 1-1-(a) and 1-6-(a) (improper financial aid, improper inducements and pre-college enrollment expenses) — The University's former head basketball coach acted in place of the University's regular scholarship awards authority by personally paying the tuition, room and board expenses of a prospective student-athlete to attend the University's summer school.

6. NCAA Constitution 3-6-(a) (ethical conduct) — (i) The involvement of the University's former head basketball coach in the violations found in this case reflects a negligible attempt on his part to operate the University's intercollegiate basketball program in accordance with NCAA regulations and (ii) The University's former head basketball coach and a former University assistant basketball coach were involved in arranging the improper transportation of a prospective student-athlete and the young man's father with full knowledge that such arrangements were contrary to NCAA legislation; further, in an attempt to cover up this violation with false and misleading information, the University's former head basketball coach requested the prospective student-athlete's father to sign a fraudulent affidavit describing this transportation.

7. NCAA Bylaw 1-1-(a) (improper inducements) — (i) The University's former head basketball coach provided the use of an automobile for approximately one week to a prospective student-athlete; (ii) On numerous occasions, the University's former head basketball coach provided the use of his outboard motorboat without charge to a prospective student-athlete; (iii) For an extended period of time during the summer and with the knowledge of the University's former head basketball coach, a prospective student-athlete received the benefit of cost-free lodging in a University dormitory; (iv) The University's former head basketball coach employed a prospective student-athlete at an excessive rate of pay to officiate a basketball scrimmage; (v) A former University assistant basketball coach gave a prospective student-athlete cash to purchase a pair of work boots and later gave the young man additional cash to spend for his own personal reasons; (vi) While on his official paid visit to the

Clemson's Penalties

University's campus, a prospective student-athlete was given three shirts by a former University assistant basketball coach; (vii) The University's former head basketball coach offered to provide a prospective student-athlete cost-free commercial airline transportation between the University and his home during his attendance at the University; (viii) A representative of the University's athletic interests gave a prospective student-athlete cash; further, the representative offered to make a substantial cash payment and provide additional cash each month during the young man's attendance at the University if he would sign a letter-of-intent; (ix) A representative of the University's athletic interests gave a prospective student-athlete cash on at least six occasions during recruiting trips to the young man's home; (x) A representative of the University's athletic interests gave a friend of a prospective student-athlete cash on at least six occasions during recruiting trips to the prospective student-athlete's home; (xi) A representative of the University's athletic interests gave cash to the father of a prospective student-athlete during a recruiting visit to the prospective student-athlete's home; (xii) While recruiting a prospective student-athlete, a representative of the University's athletic interests offered to purchase new furniture for the young man's family home, a new automobile for the young man and to make a substantial cash payment to the young man's father in exchange for a commitment to enroll in the University; (xiii) The University's former head basketball coach offered to purchase a home for the mother of a prospective student-athlete and to pay all utility bills for the home during her son's enrollment in the University; (xiv) The University's former head basketball coach gave a relative of a prospective student-athlete a substantial amount of cash to be used as a down payment for the purchase of an automobile for the prospect and subsequently gave a portion of the cash to the relative when it was returned to the coach, and (xv) The University's former head basketball coach gave a relative of a prospective student-athlete cash to pay charges incurred by the young man for lodging and a meal.

8. NCAA Bylaws 1-1-(a) and 1-5-(a) (improper inducements and entertainment) — (i) On at least three occasions, a representative of the University's athletic interests entertained a prospective student-athlete and two of his friends for dinner and, on each occasion, provided the young man cash to spend for their own personal reasons and (ii) A representative of the University's athletic interests permitted a prospective student-athlete and two of his friends to use his personal automobile at no charge to the young men for their own personal reasons; further, on at least four occasions, the representative gave the prospective student-athlete cash to pay expenses incurred while operating the automobile.

9. NCAA Bylaws 1-1-(a) and 1-6-(a) (improper inducements and pre-college enrollment expenses) (i) The University's former head basketball coach arranged for a prospective student-athlete to receive a pre-paid commercial airline ticket at no charge to the young man to travel from his home to the campus to begin summer employment and (ii) The University's former head basketball coach gave cash to a prospective student-athlete to pay the young man's automobile transportation expenses to the University in order for the young man to enroll and begin classes at the University.

10. NCAA Bylaws 1-3 and 3-2-(b) (tryouts and out-of-season basketball practice) — (i) A prospective student-athlete participated in a basketball workout with several student-athletes in the University's gymnasium; further the University's former head basketball coach and a former University assistant basketball coach observed the workout and requested the student-athletes present to evaluate the prospective student-athlete's basketball ability; (ii) A prospective student-athlete participated in a basketball workout with two student-athletes in a junior college gymnasium; further, the workout was observed by a former University assistant basketball coach, and (iii) Two prospective student-athletes participated in a basketball workout with several student-athletes in the University's gymnasium; further, the workout was observed by the University's former head basketball coach and two former University assistant basketball coaches.

11. NCAA Bylaw 1-5-(d) (improper transportation) — The University paid the commercial airline transportation costs of the parents of a prospective student-athlete to accompany the young man on his official paid visit to the University's campus.

12. NCAA Bylaw 1-5-(d)-(2) (improper transportation) — (i) The mother of a prospective student-athlete was provided transportation in a privately owned aircraft, at no cost to her, to accompany her son on his official paid visit to the University's campus, and (ii) A prospective student-athlete was transported round-trip between Clemson, South Carolina, and his home in the privately owned aircraft of a representative of the University's athletic interests who was not present during the flight; further, the young man's father was transported on this aircraft during a portion of the flight at no charge to him, and was transported at no charge round-trip in an automobile of a representative of the University's athletic interests between his home and the site where he boarded the aircraft.

13. NCAA Bylaw 1-5-(a)-(2) and 1-5-(d)-(3) (improper transportation and entertainment) — Two prospective student-athletes, their high school coaches and the parents of one of the young men were transported round-trip between the University and their homes for the young man's official paid visits in privately owned aircraft which were not accompanied by their owners; further, the high school coaches' room, board and entertainment expense during the visits were paid by the University.

14. NCAA Bylaw 1-5-(d)-(3) (improper entertainment) — The University paid the room, board and entertainment expenses of two friends of a prospective student-athlete who accompanied the young man on his second paid visit to the University's campus.

15. NCAA Bylaw 4-6-(d) (questionable practice in light of NCAA requirements) — With full knowledge on the part of the University's former head basketball coach that certain practices of the intercollegiate basketball program of the University were not in compliance with NCAA legislation, the chief executive officer of the University erroneously certified on May 9, 1974, the University's compliance with NCAA legislation.

NEWS RELEASE

THE NATIONAL COLLEGIATE ATHLETIC ASSOCIATION

U.S. Highway 50 and Nall Avenue / P.O. Box 1906 / Shawnee Mission, Kansas 66222 · 913/384-3220

Contact: Warren S. Brown

For release Tuesday p.m.s

Mailed October 6, 1975

CLEMSON UNIVERSITY PLACED ON NCAA PROBATION

MISSION. Kans.--Clemson University has been placed on probation for a period of three years for violations in the conduct of its intercollegiate basketball program it was announced today by the National Collegiate Athletic Association's Committee on Infractions.

The three-year probation includes sanctions which will prohibit the University's basketball team from participating in any postseason competition or from appearing on any NCAA-controlled television series during the probationary period.

Also, the University will be limited to awarding only two initial grants-in-aid in the sport of basketball during the 1976-77 academic year and three initial grants-in-aid during the 1977-78 academic year.

In addition, the University is publicly reprimanded for a violation occurring in the conduct of its intercollegiate football program.

Finally, in response to the "show cause" provision of the NCAA penalty structure, the University has severed all relations between certain representatives of its athletic interests and its intercollegiate athletic program.

"This case involves serious violations spanning several years and includes significant benefits and inducements to prospective and enrolled student-athletes," said Arthur R. Reynolds, chairman of the NCAA Committee on Infractions.

CLEMSON PLACED ON NCAA PROBATION
October 6, 1975
Page No. 2

"Many of the violations in this case indicate a disregard for NCAA regulations on the part of certain former athletic department staff members and athletic representatives. It is likely that more severe penalties would have been imposed without assurances from the institution that the University intends to comply fully with the governing regulations in the future," continued Reynolds.

The penalties imposed by the Committee on Infractions were for violations involving financial aid and extra benefits to student-athletes, institutional control, ethical conduct, recruiting, tryouts, entertainment, pre-college enrollment expenses, transportation, out-of-season basketball practice and a questionable practice related to the University's certification of compliance with NCAA regulations.

Following is the complete text of penalties imposed upon the institution and a summary of the violations by the University:

Penalty to be Imposed Upon Institution

1. Clemson University shall be publicly reprimanded and censured, and placed on probation for a period of three years, effective September 24, 1975, it being understood that prior to the expiration of this probationary period, the NCAA shall review the University's athletic policies and practices.

2. During the probationary period, Clemson University's intercollegiate basketball team shall end its seasons with the last, regularly scheduled, inseason contest and the University shall not be eligible to participate in the National Collegiate Basketball Championship or any other postseason basketball competition.

3. During the probationary period, Clemson University's intercollegiate basketball team shall not be eligible to appear in any television program subject to the administration and control of this Association, and the institution shall not make any commitments for such appearances during that time.

CLEMSON PLACED ON NCAA PROBATION
October 6, 1975
Page No. 3

4. During the 1976-77 academic year, no more than two student-athletes in
    the sport of basketball shall receive initial, athletically related fi-
    nancial aid (as set forth in O.I. 500) which has been arranged for or
    awarded by Clemson University.

5. During the 1977-78 academic year, no more than three student-athletes
    in the sport of basketball shall receive initial, athletically related,
    financial aid (as set forth in O.I. 500) which has been arranged for or
    awarded by Clemson University.

6. Clemson University shall be publicly reprimanded for a recruiting viola-
    tion occurring in the conduct of its intercollegiate football program.

7. In accordance with action taken by Clemson University in response to the
    "show cause" provision of the NCAA penalty structure, the University's
    intercollegiate athletic program shall completely sever all relations,
    whether formal or informal, with certain representatives of the Univer-
    sity's athletic interests involved in violations of NCAA legislation
    in this case including, but not limited to, the representatives' finan-
    cial support, recruiting efforts and membership in institutional booster
    groups.

Violations of NCAA Legislation

1. NCAA Constitution 3-1-(a)-(3), 3-1-(g)-(6) and 3-4-(a) [amateurism and
    student participation, extra benefits and improper financial aid to
    student-athletes] -- The University's former head basketball coach gave
    a student-athlete cash in excess of face value for the sale of his two
    Atlantic Coast Conference basketball tournament ticket books.

2. NCAA Constitution 3-1-(g)-(6) and 3-4-(a) [extra benefits and improper
    financial aid to student-athletes] -- (i) On numerous occasions, the Uni-
    versity's former head basketball coach and a former assistant basketball
    coach gave cash in small amounts to certain members of the University's
    intercollegiate basketball team to spend for their own personal reasons;
    (ii) The University's former head basketball coach paid a telephone bill
    charged to a student-athlete at no expense to the young man; (iii) The
    University's former head basketball coach paid, with his own personal
    funds, charges for work performed on a student-athlete's personal automo-
    bile, and (iv) The University's former head basketball coach paid, with
    his own personal funds, the balance of two bank loans on behalf of a
    student-athlete.

CLEMSON PLACED ON NCAA PROBATION
October 6, 1975
Page No. 4

3. NCAA Constitution 3-1-(g)-(5), 3-1-(g)-(6) and 3-4-(a) [improper expenses, extra benefits and improper financial aid to student-athletes] -- (i) Through the arrangements of the University's former head basketball coach, a student-athlete received the benefit of round-trip commercial airline transportation at no charge to the young man between Greenville, South Carolina, and his home; (ii) The University's former head basketball coach gave a student-athlete cash to pay the young man's round-trip commercial airline transportation charges between Greenville, South Carolina, and his home, and (iii) Through the arrangements of the University's former head basketball coach and his personal secretary, a student-athlete received the benefits of round-trip commercial airline transportation between Greenville, South Carolina, and his home at no charge to the young man.

4. NCAA Constitution 3-2 [institutional control] -- The involvement of certain representatives of the University's athletic interests in the violations set forth in this case demonstrates that Clemson University did not adequately exercise institutional control and responsibility over these individuals.

5. NCAA Constitution 3-4-(a) and Bylaws 1-1-(a) and 1-6-(a) [improper financial aid, improper inducements and pre-college enrollment expenses] -- The University's former head basketball coach acted in place of the University's regular scholarship awards authority by personally paying the tuition, room and board expenses of a prospective student-athlete to attend the University's summer school.

6. NCAA Constitution 3-6-(a) [ethical conduct] -- (i) The involvement of the University's former head basketball coach in the violations found in this case reflects a negligible attempt on his part to operate the University's intercollegiate basketball program in accordance with NCAA regulations and (ii) The University's former head basketball coach and a former University assistant basketball coach were involved in arranging the improper transportation of a prospective student-athlete and the young man's father with full knowledge that such arrangements were contrary to NCAA legislation; further, in an attempt to cover up this violation with false and misleading information, the University's former head basketball coach requested the prospective student-athlete's father to sign a fraudulent affidavit describing this transportation.

7. NCAA Bylaw 1-1-(a) [improper inducements] -- (i) The University's former head basketball coach provided the use of an automobile for approximately one week to a prospective student-athlete; (ii) On numerous occasions, the University's former head basketball coach provided the use of his outboard motorboat without charge to a prospective student-athlete;

CLEMSON PLACED ON NCAA PROBATION
October 6, 1975
Page No. 5

_____

(iii) For an extended period of time during the summer and with the knowledge of the University's former head basketball coach, a prospective student-athlete received the benefit of cost-free lodging in a University dormitory; (iv) The University's former head basketball coach employed a prospective student-athlete at an excessive rate of pay to officiate a basketball scrimmage; (v) A former University assistant basketball coach gave a prospective student-athlete cash to purchase a pair of work boots and later gave the young man additional cash to spend for his own personal reasons; (vi) While on his official paid visit to the University's campus, a prospective student-athlete was given three shirts by a former University assistant basketball coach; (vii) The University's former head basketball coach offered to provide a prospective student-athlete cost-free commercial airline transportation between the University and his home during his attendance at the University; (viii) A representative of the University's athletic interests gave a prospective student-athlete cash; further, the representative offered to make a substantial cash payment and provide additional cash each month during the young man's attendance at the University if he would sign a letter-of-intent; (ix) A representative of the University's athletic interests gave a prospective student-athlete cash on at least six occasions during recruiting trips to the young man's home; (x) A representative of the University's athletic interests gave a friend of a prospective student-athlete cash on at least six occasions during recruiting trips to the prospective student-athlete's home; (xi) A representative of the University's athletic interests gave cash to the father of a prospective student-athlete during a recruiting visit to the prospective student-athlete's home; (xii) While recruiting a prospective student-athlete, a representative of the University's athletic interests offered to purchase new furniture for the young man's family home, a new automobile for the young man and to make a substantial cash payment to the young man's father in exchange for a commitment to enroll in the University; (xiii) The University's former head basketball coach offered to purchase a house for the mother of a prospective student-athlete and to pay all utility bills for the home during her son's enrollment in the University; (xiv) The University's former head basketball coach gave a relative of a prospective student-athlete a substantial amount of cash to be used as a down payment for the purchase of an automobile for the prospect and subsequently gave a portion of the cash to the relative when it was returned to the coach, and (xv) The University's former head basketball coach gave a relative of a prospective student-athlete cash to pay charges incurred by the young man for lodging and a meal.

128

CLEMSON PLACED ON NCAA PROBATION
October 6, 1975
Page No. 6

8. NCAA Bylaws 1-1-(a) and 1-5-(e) [improper inducements and entertainment] --
    (i) On at least three occasions, a representative of the University's
    athletic interests entertained a prospective student-athlete and two of
    his friends·for dinner and, on each occasion, provided the young men
    cash to spend for their own personal reasons and (ii) A representative
    of the University's athletic interests permitted a prospective student-
    athlete and two of his friends to use his personal automobile at no charge
    to the young men for their own personal reasons; further, on at least
    four occasions, the representative gave the prospective student-athlete
    cash to pay expenses incurred while operating the automobile.

9. NCAA Bylaws 1-1-(a) and 1-6-(a) [improper inducements and pre-college en-
    rollment expenses] -- (i) The University's former head basketball coach
    arranged for a prospective student-athlete to receive a pre-paid commer-
    cial airline ticket at no charge to the young man to travel from his home
    to the campus to begin summer employment and (ii) The University's former
    head basketball coach gave cash to a prospective student-athlete to pay
    the young man's automobile transportation expenses to the University in
    order for the young man to enroll and begin classes at the University.

10. NCAA Bylaws 1-3 and 3-2-(b) [tryouts and out-of-season basketball prac-
    tice] -- (i) A prospective student-athlete participated in a basketball
    workout with several student-athletes in the University's gymnasium;
    further, the University's former head basketball coach and a former Uni-
    versity assistant basketball coach observed the workout and requested
    the student-athletes present to evaluate the prospective student-athlete's
    basketball ability; (ii) A prospective student-athlete participated in a
    basketball workout with two student-athletes in a junior college gymnasium;
    further, the workout was observed by a former University assistant basket-
    ball coach, and (iii) Two prospective student-athletes participated in
    a basketball workout with several student-athletes in the University's
    gymnasium; further, the workout was observed by the University's former
    head basketball coach and two former University assistant basketball
    coaches.

11. NCAA Bylaw 1-5-(d) [improper transportation] -- The University paid the
    commercial airline transportation costs of the parents of a prospective
    student-athlete to accompany the young man on his official paid visit to
    the University's campus.

12. NCAA Bylaw 1-5-(d)-(2) [improper transportation] -- (i) The mother of
    a prospective student-athlete was provided transportation in a privately
    owned aircraft, at no cost to her, to accompany her son on his official
    paid visit to the University's campus, and (ii) A prospective student-
    athlete was transported round-trip between Clemson, South Carolina, and
    his home in the privately owned aircraft of a representative of the Uni-
    versity's athletic interests who was not present during the flight;

CLEMSON PLACED ON NCAA PROBATION
October 6, 1975
Page No. 7

further, the young man's father was transported on this aircraft during
a portion of the flight at no charge to him, and was transported at
no charge round-trip in an automobile of a representative of the University's athletic interests between his home and the site where he
boarded the aircraft.

13. NCAA Bylaw 1-5-(d)-(2) and 1-5-(d)-(3) [improper transportation and
entertainment] -- Two prospective student-athletes, their high school
coaches and the parents of one of the young men were transported round-
trip between the University and their homes for the young men's official
paid visits in privately owned aircrafts which were not accompanied by
their owners; further, the high school coaches' room, board and entertainment expenses during the visits were paid by the University.

14. NCAA Bylaw 1-5-(d)-(3) [improper entertainment] -- The University paid
the room, board and entertainment expenses of two friends of a prospective student-athlete who accompanied the young man on his second paid visit
to the University's campus.

15. NCAA Bylaw 4-6-(d) [questionable practice in light of NCAA requirements] --
With full knowledge on the part of the University's former head basketball coach that certain practices of the intercollegiate basketball program of the University were not in compliance with NCAA legislation, the
chief executive officer of the University erroneously certified on May 9,
1974, the University's compliance with NCAA legislation.

12
LADY LOCKE

"I don't think he knew what he was going up against," recalled Nancy Locke, sitting in the living room of their Jacksonville beach home in the spring of 1981. "All he could think about when he came to Clemson that first year (1970-71 season) was that he had finally made it to the ACC. He thought that league was tops.

"There's no doubt in my mind it was...and is...a good league but the situation at Clemson hardly rivaled the quality of the ACC. I mean, I remember the day of his very first game, we got a telephone call. I picked up the phone and it was a man, a stranger. He said, "I just want to tell you to tell your husband that if there are more than three blacks playing at any one time, during any game, you better hope your children are not playing in the streets."

"That was the first threatening phone call...the first of many. I guess you could say we always lived somewhat in fear of what could happen. Our two sons, John and Mike, were four and two at the time. Kathy, our youngest, had been born only the spring before (April 2, 1970). I felt like any mother would have felt—concerned.

"I believe one of the things which got Tates into some of his problems at Clemson was that he had had too much success too soon in his career. At West Point he had gone to the NIT twice; at Miami he had gone to the NIT and also the NCAA tournament. Everything had sort of fallen into place— Tates never had to fight for it.

"That's why he went down the tube at Clemson. He couldn't stand it not being easy. So he started to do some things that I'm sure he wasn't proud of, things that would make winning easier. Oh, he never actually came home and told me he was cheating—or bending the rules—but once he started bringing people like B.C. Inabinet and those others around the house you'd have to be a fool not to know. Those people told him things he wanted to hear. They could do this for him or they could do that. He was swayed by them. Tates is a very gullible person.

"He just couldn't stand the thought of losing and I don't think he knew just how bad off Clemson's program was, compared to the rest of the league, when he got the job. After the losses started coming in that first and second year—and with those bad influences around—he just lost all perspective.

"Then he lost his self-respect, and when you lose that you lose everything. If you don't respect yourself you can't respect anybody else. I think what happened after that was he got deeper and deeper into the situation. There was no turning back, so I guess he figured 'What the heck'. He decided to ride the ship to the bottom.

"The town of Clemson, itself, wasn't bad. We lived out in the country—it doesn't take long to get to the country when you're in Clemson. Our house was in a section called Camelot, at 109 Knight Circle. No, it wasn't named after Bobby Knight...I guess Tates just can't separate himself from the name.

"Like I said, we were comfortable. We had four bedrooms, a family room and a finished basement. Back then we bought it for about $60,000, so I know it's got be close to $100,000 or more on today's market.

"When Tates used to talk about the 'Clemson Family' I used to laugh. That was a joke. I don't mean Tates' assistants and their wives; there wasn't a wife I didn't get along with. I'm talking about the Clemson administration. Most of those people were a bunch of phony baloneys. People like Walter Cox, the vice president of student affairs. And athletic director Bill McLellan. They were two of the biggest phonies.

"I think the 'Clemson Family' looked upon Tates as what he was, not who he was. There was no personal concern about him, if you know what I mean. They just wanted to use him for their own, selfish reasons...and Tates let them.

"When the NCAA investigation began, when all the problems came out, the Clemson administration turned their backs on Tates. I guess it's human nature to do that. They really bailed out. The whole scene was an emotional mess. The year before assistant coach George Hill bailed out...then Cliff Malpass, the other assistant, was next. And I don't really blame them. They weren't happy there.

"One of the things I can be thankful for, I guess, is that my kids didn't have to live through all that turmoil. They were too small to really understand. Even today, they still don't know what happened except that their father cheated as a basketball coach and got caught.

"Both John and Mike love their father...Kathy, too. The two boys just worship Tates. Mike is the basketball player of the two, but John has enjoyed working with Tates when he was at Jacksonville, just doing some odd jobs for the team and sitting on the bench as a team manager. Both John and Mike live and die for the game—just like Tates. And Kathy? Well, she cries when they lose a game. She's into the sport.

"You know, it's funny, I've always enjoyed watching basketball and I've tried to support Tates in his chosen profession, although I know some of his friends will tell you I've been a negative influence. The nagging wife, you know. That's not it...I really do want him to be a basketball coach.

"Tates loves coaching; he loves kids. The game is his life. I don't think there is any question that he wanted to do anything else, though his father, I'm sure, had other ideas. I think Mr. Locke wanted him to be a manufacturer's representative, go into the business with him. That's not for Tates. He tried it after he got fired by the Buffalo Braves and he found out it wasn't his cup of tea. Basketball is. It's his life, the first and singlemost important thing.

"People ask me if I knew what I was getting into when I married Tates in 1960. I believe I did. I was a student at Ohio Wesleyan when I met him during my sophomore year in 1958. I was majoring in education and Tates, who was a senior, was majoring in physical education. He didn't make the basketball team at Miami of Ohio, so he transferred to Ohio Wesleyan after his sophomore year. At Ohio Wesleyan he made the basketball team and became captain but that wasn't something I knew about until after I met him. Actually, I had no idea who he was or what he did. In fact, I never, ever saw him play a game.

"Tates was 22 at the time; I was two years younger. He was an intense fella, but he liked to have a good time. He liked to go to concerts. He was sort of a rebel for his time.

"I remember the night he took me to a Louis Armstrong concert. Everybody was all dressed up but here comes Tates, wearing blue jeans and a tee shirt. We went to the back of the chapel, where the concert was being held, and sat on the windowsill. While everyone else sat there quietly, Tates really let it go. He got up and clapped and screamed...he really let it go. He had a good ol' time.

"Actually, the wildest thing about him was the black '57 Chevy with red interior that he drove. He used to race that car. Thought he was big time, too.

"My parents thought Tates was awful. Why? Because he showed up to meet them the first time in the same outfit he wore to the Louis Armstrong concert. And he didn't even wear any socks, just sneakers.

"Tates liked to give people the impression he was a jock and a person who loved to have fun. I'll give you another example. There was a time at Ohio Wesleyan when he thought it would be funny to make an impromptu appearance in the classroom one day. The classroom was right next to the men's locker room so Tates hustled in there, took off all his clothes and walked back into class with only a jock strap, a baseball hat and a pair of galoshes.

"It was a *coed* class. He hadn't counted on that. Well, he died and turned a thousand colors and turned around and walked out. That was even worse, when he turned around. That's Tates, having a good time. He's unconventional but he thoroughly enjoys living every day.

"I was still going to school when we got married in July of 1960. Tates had stayed around my junior year, working as the assistant coach of the school team. I really didn't want to finish, because Tates had taken the assistant's job at West Point, but I had to promise my parents that I'd get my degree or else they wouldn't sign the papers for me to get married.

"So I promised them. Of course, at the time, I had no intention of going through with it...returning to school. But Tates made me. He put me on a plane out of New York City and I finished my education.

"Discussing the wedding reminds me of our honeymoon. Tates invited his army buddy and his wife to join us at Lake Cumberland in Kentucky. Oh yeah, the guy also brought along his beagle dog. That's how our marriage began—we went fishing in Kentucky, the four of us and the dog.

"That should have told me something right then.

"I really enjoyed most of the time at West Point, especially the early years there when Tates was an assistant coach. It was an exciting life for a 22-year-old. We were young and having a good time. Once he got the head coach job in 1963, we moved onto the post. It was different then, because we were civilians on a military base and a lot of them resented us. We lived in the Athletic Association triplex. It was us, the trainer and the assistant football coach.

"It was while at Army that Tates hooked up with Bobby Knight, who became his assistant coach (in 1963-64 and 1964-65) and then succeeded Tates when he left. I can't pinpoint the exact date Tates met Bobby...he just seems like he's always been around, if you know what I mean.

"I've always liked Bobby. He and Tates are so much alike. For instance, Bobby is a chauvinist, but so is Tates. He has no use for women as people but he's very influenced by them.

"When we left Army and Bobby Knight we moved on to Miami of Ohio. Moved into a teeny-weeny house the first year we were there while our home was being built. That tiny house which we rented was terrible but it was fun. We didn't care. I was teaching at the time and at the end of our first year we moved into the other house.

"Life was pretty good to us in those years. Tates was still a fun person to be around but it was about this time he started to develop these superstitions. He had this one...well, it was crazy. This one particular season we had a lot of close games. In one game the score was getting close again, so Tates called a time out. He sent his manager over to get me and take me out of the gym. Tates wanted me to leave because I had been to so many of the close games he lost. So I guess this would change his luck.

"I out-smarted him, though. We won the game but I never left. Oh, I got up and left my seat, but I walked down to the lower level and stood by the door, right behind where the team sat, so Tates wouldn't see me. He came home that night and said, 'See, it worked'. I don't know if he ever found out that I didn't leave, but he never asked me to leave again after that.

"That was the only way he got on me in those days. He never really got nasty, got uptight about things, until the second or third year at Clemson. In the beginning, I didn't know he was drinking or popping diet pills, but I knew *something* was going on because his behavior had changed. He was very uptight about everything. Sometimes you couldn't talk to him at all.

"I remember this one time I wanted to get my hair frosted. Apparently he didn't want me to. He said, 'No, you're not getting it frosted.' I said, 'But I really want to.' Then he shouted, 'You're not doing it because it's my money.'

"That just took my breath away. He had never talked to me like that before. By then, I knew the pressure was getting to him. The team had gone 9-17 the first year and then 10-16. I noticed that it didn't take as much to rattle him. The kids started to get on his nerves and they had never bothered him before.

"We moved to a larger house, in Camelot, but things didn't improve. He began coming home later and later. There was more alcohol in the house and sometimes he'd sit there and drink scotch and milk, one right after the other. I think he got the habit from Tree Rollins' mother. I thought it was disgusting. Tates never really got drunk, to the point of passing out, but he did get a loose tongue.

"Then there were the diet pills. I could tell when he was doing those. He would either be kind of slow in his speech or his words would come out hysterically, even in normal conversation. He didn't think I knew about the pills and would deny using them every time I questioned him about it. But I knew better. It wasn't until later, when he felt all the trouble around him in 1975 at Clemson, that he admitted to me about taking those pills.

"The drinking and pill-popping were only part of our problems. Tates was also out on the streets, running around with the boys at night. And with some women, too. It was in the fall of 1974, I believe, when I got a phone call from someone who had seen Tates out with this woman. I approached him about it but naturally he denied having anything to do with her.

"But I wondered.

"Then I started getting phone calls from the woman. She'd call our home and hang up. I knew who it was. I'm not stupid. I just didn't know who it was until much later.

"It was around this time that I had my breakdown. I had kept everything inside and was having trouble getting to sleep. I'd be waiting up till all hours of the morning for Tates to come home. That's when I turned to the pills—the sleeping pills, for help. Pretty soon one pill wasn't enough. I needed two...then three. You know how it goes. Finally, I cracked up.

"It was in January of 1975, that last season at Clemson. They had to put me in the hospital for 10 days. I don't think you'd term it a total nervous breakdown—I mean, I still knew who I was—but I could feel this constant, unrelenting anxiety.

"You might have thought my hospitalization would have snapped Tates back to reality but it didn't. He was still running around, still drinking and popping diet pills.

"But I still stayed loyal to him. I was so loyal to him that when I was in that hospital, when the doctors were trying to help me get myself back together, I never told them what was really bothering me. At that point I didn't trust anybody, I was afraid one of the doctors or someone would go and give the information to the NCAA or something. So I was loyal to him, even to the point of risking my health.

"It was probably too late for Tates to recognize this...to even care. The shadiness of the situation at Clemson had turned around his whole personality. He didn't respect me; he didn't respect himself. It just destroyed him, ate him alive. He wasn't the same man I had married in 1960."

13
A CAUTIOUS
COMEBACK

The most difficult thing for me to realize following my dismissal at Clemson was the simple fact that I had not done anything illegal. At least not according to the way our country's laws read. What I was guilty of was strictly a professional immorality, not something socially immoral or illegal.

Regardless, I still felt like a crook, like a cheat. I guess when you bring shame and ugliness to a sport that you really love, the hurt and guilt runs deep. When I got caught I felt like a guy who had just been pulled over by the police for speeding. You know the feeling—everyone on the highway passes by and stares at you. Frankly, you're embarrassed. That's how I felt, amplified many times over. Even the telephone calls from my friends didn't help me to get over this total feeling of embarassment.

Some periods of April were worse than others, like when I had to be out in public. Then I couldn't hide. One of the most difficult things I did that spring was attend a YMCA banquet in Spartanburg, South Carolina and introduce Bobby Knight to over 1,000 people. It was very tough on me emotionally but somehow I got through it.

Shortly after I was invited to speak at another banquet in the state. This was an all-star basketball affair in Greenville, put on by the high school coaches association, a group which I had helped organize during my tenure at Clemson, much to the chagrin of the high school athletic association. The coaches association was more or less a bastard outfit with the central idea being unification of the coaches. It took them two years, but now the group was solid.

I had consented to speak at their banquet before the roof fell in on me at school. Later, I tried to beg out of the commitment but the association's president wouldn't hear of it. They still wanted me as their speaker.

So I came. Unfortunately, the banquet only lowered my spirits. As I stood before the group, only then did it really dawn on me what damage I had done at Clemson. Not only did I destroy myself, but I had left a black mark on the game of basketball itself. I had cast a shadow over a sport I dearly loved, just to help one school get ahead.

I felt ashamed of myself. I guess somewhere along the line I had forgotten basketball is much bigger than one particular school...it is much larger than the people who make it up. Certainly, basketball is much larger than one coach.

For a month after that engagement I went into a state of total depression. For most of May I hid from the eye of the public.

I had broken a sacred trust basketball people are supposed to have for others in the game. At the Greenville banquet, they had presented me with an award, the only trophy which has ever meant anything to me. As I was receiving it, I looked out into the audience at all the faces, all the people I had let down. At young kids who had attended my summer camps; at other coaches; at mothers and fathers who had trusted me with their sons. All those people had put their trust in me and I had let them down.

I felt so helpless, a feeling rather unique for me because in the past I had always been able to face frustration and failure and see the light at the end of the tunnel. This time I didn't see that light...I only saw darkness.

It was about that time that I received a telephone call from the head coach of the Buffalo Braves. Jack Ramsay said he was interested in having me come aboard as his assistant coach. I listened.

It was a big boost hearing from Jack, a man whom I had admired for many years dating all the way back to my coaching days at West Point. I remember driving four or five hours from the Point to Philadelphia to watch Jack's St. Joseph's team. I was always intrigued with the way Ramsay changed his defenses during a game. He was a master at switching defenses, but I don't think he ever received enough credit for his contribution to the sport.

Yeah, Jack was my idol and it was like a dream come true when he phoned. If nothing else, it helped momentarily to make me forget some of the garbage dumped on me at Clemson.

I told Jack I needed to discuss the move with Nancy before I could give him an answer.

When we made the move from Miami of Ohio to Clemson in 1970 it was done against Nancy's will. She liked the lifestyle in Oxford, Ohio. It was a pace she was more at ease with socially, quite unlike the demands we had at West Point. That was my major reason for leaving the Point—Nancy had a breakdown.

At Clemson I lost touch with my values. Stuff was just laying there. Money came easy and so did the women. There were alumni wives who were quite open about their personal need for affection, not just for me but for members of my staff. I couldn't believe it; I had never been a part of anything like this before. After I married Nancy and all through my years at West Point and Miami, I wouldn't even consider looking at another woman. It was the way I was brought up. But my values changed almost overnight at Clemson.

The pressures from losing in my first two or three years made me an easy target, I guess. I was drinking too much scotch, popping too many pills. Life was moving too fast for this small town guy to handle. My values slipped and slipped and slipped and the people who got hurt were my family.

We had some family problems after we adopted the two boys, but those problems could be attributed to basketball, not booze, pills and women. I was a dedicated basketball coach, married to my job. Even today, unfortunately, my job still comes first...except if there is sickness in my family. Then I stop. But I go right back to basketball as soon as the crisis is over.

Everybody says there's God, your family and your job. I love my job first. I don't know why, but it's true. My children come next. I tried to understand why I'm like this and I guess it's because I find women very selfish. I find them very amenable to what you want to hear during the period of time when they feel they have an opportunity to be a part of your life. I have found once they're there, then this attitude changes tremendously.

Man will bust his ass—say the right things or anything else—to get a woman into bed. But once he's obtained his goal, he will return to real life and work hard. A woman wants much more than that. She wants to put her tentacles around the man. She wants a lot of self control within that person to help carry out the whole nine yards, for better or worse.

It takes a special woman to have a life of her own and still be a part of a man's life...and live life to its fullest. It takes a special woman. I don't know of a woman today that I can point to and say, 'there she is.' Maybe I know one, but I don't know her well enough to say that.

Nancy never understood my feelings on the subject and she had a difficult time adjusting to being the wife of a college basketball coach. The wife of a coach has to live with that guy's ego; she has to accept his workaholic attitude and his desire to be a success. And she has to accept losing a good part of her own identity. She becomes known as Mrs. Tates Locke, not Nancy Locke. It takes a tough woman to stay out there and be herself and not be in conflict or in competition with him. Nancy is a withdrawn person and it wasn't easy for her.

She was pampered, babied and never given any discipline as a child. She was the oldest of three children and always had a grandmother taking care of her all the time. I was an only child. My mom had an eighth grade education and my father a high school education. I had to work hard since I was a kid—I don't remember not having a job. There was always work to do, so what's the big deal?

Nancy was a terrible housekeeper. Why? Well, she was never taught how. So a lot of these things added up to create tension in our relationship. I had never grown up in a sloppy house and it pissed me off to find myself, and my kids, living this way. I've never understood why people can't pick up after themselves. Later on, even at Jacksonville, that's what led to our splitting up. Housekeeping, that was the thing. I couldn't stand it after 15 years.

I decided to try and resolve things with Nancy and patch up our home life. After some discussion, she agreed to come with me to Buffalo. In the meantime, before reaching my decision in June, I fished almost every day with Charlie Harrison and my son John. Some real weird things happened to me.

There were occasions I got so drunk I didn't remember anything for days. One time we were out fishing and I stood up in the boat to take a piss. I was so intoxicated I fell overboard.

I was also having a lot of nightmares and had trouble staying awake while driving at night. I even thought about committing suicide, but it never got beyond that stage. I never actually attempted to take my own life. I still believed life was worth living, else God wouldn't have put me on this earth. I decided I had created much of the mess I was in and that I would have to fight my way back.

We held my summer basketball camp, Bill Clendinen and I, and made enough money to pay off my debt to the IRS and a few other friends. Then I called Jack Ramsay and accepted his offer.

We left for Buffalo in August. I sold everything, including the house and extra car. We made a clean break. I knew I wanted to remain in basketball in some capacity and Jack was giving me an opportunity, even if it was in professional basketball. The NBA had never appealed to me—and I told Jack that—but he convinced me I could do a job for him.

I soon found out differently.

"Tates was naive about many of the things which went on in the NBA," explained Ramsay. "What a coach in our league has to understand is that you have a particular roster of players who will be with you for an entire season. You have to find a way to live with them. By the time a player gets to the NBA you're not going to be able to change his ways significantly. Or his personality. So it's a matter of blending these people into a team which is going to be able to beat another team. It's much different from college ball."

Jack was so right.

But Jack Ramsay was different. Jack has the ability to bounce back after a bad defeat. He can see frustration or failure and get away by himself and the next day he's okay again. Not me. I never had the feel for the pro game and it wasn't until probably my third year at Jacksonville University that I learned to cope with defeat. Cope with it, not accept it.

But in Buffalo it was different. I took every loss badly. Every one.

The NBA is a show, an act. It's like being in a circus and people come to watch you perform. Every ballplayer, it seemed, wanted to go out on the court and put on a big show. Everybody was overpaid and they all were out there trying to outdo the next guy.

There were some fun times. The conglomerate of people the Braves had were really good people. They were fun to be around. There was never any doubt that the Buffalo owner, Paul Snyder, was in another world. He was short and stocky and his ego was the size of Buffalo. He lived like he was in Disneyland and everybody else lived someplace else.

He had made his fortune in the frozen food industry, working very hard but always doing things *his* way. You worked for him and you became totally enslaved to the guy. There was a certain fear...he stomped his foot and you jumped high in the air. Maybe that worked for him in the frozen food business but watching him try to run an NBA team the same way was funny.

Jack Ramsay was different. He's a neat guy. He has certain rules you live by, rules that are fairly simple. He expects you to live by those rules but he's not a policeman. Basically all he asks is for a player to go hard, keep the pressure on your opponent, not your own people. So you had Jack's philosophy on one hand and Snyder's theories on the other.

You could see it would be a hard mix, especially with the bunch of players they had on that club, guys who were put together with glue and bailing wire. We had Randy Smith, Ken Charles, Jim McMillian, Bob McAdoo, Bobby Weiss, Garfield Heard, Dale Schlueter, Jack Marin, Tom McMillen and Ernie DiGregorio. It was quite a cast of characters, all of them fine people with unique personalities.

Marin had the greatest sense of humor of any man I've known. Weiss was very intelligent—he knew some of the best coin tricks around. Then there was Bob McAdoo. I know Mac has been bad-mouthed a lot over the years but to me he was a beautiful person, one who had been totally misunderstood.

Jack Ramsay knew how to get the most out of Mac—he was the kind of guy you played right *at* offensively. Other coaches have made the mistake of trying to play him differently in their offense and it doesn't work. I knew poor Mac was headed for his death when we dealt him to the New York Knicks at the beginning of my second year in Buffalo. That was his death. After leading the NBA in scoring for three straight seasons, including the 1975-76 campaign, McAdoo hasn't been heard from since.

What a competitor he was, even in practice. The fact he is sour these days is rather sad. He was dealt a bad deal. All Mac ever wanted from Buffalo was to be treated with the same financial respect the club afforded Ernie D. Ernie DiGregorio was making more money than he was worth dead—I think it was something like two million bucks over 20 years.

Don't misunderstand, I didn't dislike Ernie. I mean, he was great with my kids. I just never liked the way Ernie played basketball. For him to help your club he needed a great supporting cast. If things didn't go his way, he would sit on the bench and pout. I can still see Ernie now, down at the other end, with that damn white towel over his head.

As a person he didn't bother me. I liked him. But a coach has the right not to like a ballplayer, just as the player has the same right not to like the coach. It works both ways. Ernie never got along with me because Ernie never got along with anybody who did not see things his way. I wouldn't let DiGregorio do his thing and that bothered him. He had been spoiled.

Being associated with this circus was constant laughs. Even our trainer, Ray Melchiorre, was a terribly funny guy with a dry sense of humor. I don't think I would have survived my rookie year in the NBA if it hadn't been for Ray.

He was the kind of guy who didn't run the streets, so for Ray to walk up to a stewardess in an airport and say, 'Hi, my name is Ray, how do you like me so far?' was terribly funny. I always looked forward to Ray's impromptu airport introductions.

Sometimes the players pulled jokes on me, like when they got me lost inside the Dallas airport and ran off. It was something different every day. I'm sure Ramsay enjoyed having me around, but I was probably more of a pain in the ass than I was a help to him. Life in the pros was a big joke.

Sometimes, however, the jokes weren't so funny.

The day after Buffalo lost to the Boston Celtics in the Eastern Conference finals, four games to two, the Braves fired Ramsay. They made it look like it was the losses to Boston, but Jack had taken Buffalo about as far as the club could go. The real reason Jack wasn't rehired was money—Ramsay was making over $100,000. Snyder thought he could save $60,000.

He offered me the job. I asked Jack for his advice. He said, "Tates, don't take it. They're only gonna make a monkey out of you."

I didn't listen. I saw it as my chance to be the head coach of an NBA club, or as Randy Smith put it, "the head mutherfucker." In reality, I wasn't prepared for the pros but I bowed to my enthusiasm and cockiness and signed with the Braves for $40,000. After a season under Ramsay, I figured what else was there to learn?

Well, as I soon found out, there was *plenty* to learn.

That summer the Braves' owners put the club—and me—in a terrible hole by trading away some of the players with large salaries. It was strictly an economy move and it shouldn't have been that surprising, considering the rumors surrounding a relocation of the franchise to Hollywood, Florida.

Kenny Charles, a good backup guard, was traded and so was small forward Jim McMillian, who went to the Knicks for $400,000.

Compounding the problem was a sudden change in philosophy at the NBA draft in June. We had spent almost $80,000 following Indiana's star guard Quinn Buckner around the country. I even saw him play in Hawaii. The kid was great; he was just what we needed in our backcourt to get the ball inside to McAdoo.

But we didn't draft Buckner. At the last minute I got a call from the owners, Snyder and John Y. Brown, telling me they wanted to select Notre Dame forward Adrian Dantley. It shocked me. I knew Adrian was a good player—his NBA offensive statistics support it—but we already had McMillian as our big forward. What we needed was a guard, not another small forward. We needed Buckner to solve another problem—getting rid of Ernie D.

Snyder and Brown would not budge, so we selected Dantley. I was pissed. Then about six weeks later, adding insult to injury, we sent McMillian off to New York before signing Dantley. What a dumb move. I knew Adrian's agent, Donald Dell, because he also represented Tom McMillen. I knew Dell was tough, so by selling McMillian before we signed Dantley we played right into Dell's wallet.

It proved to be only the beginning of the nightmare.

We began the 1976 exhibition season on a high note, winning a slew of games and finishing with the club's best pre-season record in history. Our good fortunes continued into the regular season with wins over Boston, Philadelphia and Denver. But we went out to the West Coast and got pummeled...lost in overtime to Houston and San Antonio, then got crushed in Los Angeles and Portland. Now we were struggling.

Our opponents had begun to take advantage of Dantley's inexperience. One predicament lead to another. Dissension set in. Next we sold McAdoo and McMillen to the Knicks in December for John Gianelli and cash. I couldn't believe it. Neither could my assistant coach Charlie. That's right, the same Charlie Harrison. I had rescued his ass from the European leagues over the summer.

After we dealt away McAdoo December 9, Harrison laid the same line on me as I had told him after the N. C. State game two years before.

"Coach, it's over. Call off the dogs. We're dead"

By the end of December our record was 14-20.

Meanwhile, while we were waiting for the ax to fall on our necks, John Y. was wheeling and dealing, brought in some real driftwood. Guys like Bird Averitt and Johnny Neumann. Every day, it seemed, there was a new face in camp. Brown had general manager Bob MacKinnon around his finger—he was a puppet—so there was no opposition. Brown was destroying the club.

Our roster looked like a Salvation Army Team, filled with players who had bounced all around the NBA. Buffalo soon became a spot to hold tryout camps. We were a dropoff area for the other clubs. No wonder our offense looked like a Chinese firedrill.

I wasn't a basketball coach, but a guy hanging out. That's all I was doing. It was unreal. On top of all this, I had to look down the end of the bench and watch Ernie D. sulk. I could have used Ernie's white towel for something more appropriate—like a surrender.

By January we were getting killed every time we stepped onto the court and I knew it wouldn't be long before Brown and friends handed me my walking papers. I knew MacKinnon had the inside word, but he swore he didn't know. Of course, he was lying.

Finally, the inevitable came. We went on the road and lost in Kansas City, 132-104. We played in Denver and got trounced, 127-107. After the January 24 game we flew back to Buffalo and the next day the Braves scheduled a press conference. You can bet I knew what that was for.

The statement said briefly: "Tates Locke has been relieved of his coaching duties." They were right about one thing: I *was* relieved—about getting out of Buffalo. Unfortunately, that also meant I was unemployed again.

When I walked out of the Braves' front offices that day I wondered if I would ever get another shot in basketball. I mean, I was a disgrace *everywhere*. I didn't know what to do, who to turn to. Oh, a few NBA people like Eddie Donovan and Stu Inman offered their help, but I was sour on the NBA. I was sour on everything in life.

I realized then, as I do now, I had made a dumb mistake by not listening to Ramsay. He had predicted everything. He had been right on every point. I did become nothing more than a monkey in Buffalo.

Actually, I had wanted to stay with Jack, but he wasn't sure about taking the head coaching spot with the Portland Trailblazers. It wasn't until after I committed myself with the Braves that Jack took the position. It's ironic how it worked out. Jack went to Portland and they went on to win the NBA championship; I stayed in Buffalo, the team went 17-30, and I was out on my ass by mid-January.

I realize now I wasn't ready to handle the players, general managers or owners in the NBA. When to read them and when not to read them. I soon learned there are only a few solid NBA organizations which allow basketball people to make decisions. Everybody else walks a tightrope.

I had foolishly assumed it would be like college basketball, where you would be allowed to do what you thought was best for your program. That wasn't the case in the NBA. Owners are on a tremendous ego trip and all too often they allow friends or business associates in other fields to get involved in the operation of the ballclub. I remember Snyder allowed a food broker friend to take over as the Braves' business manager. That was the crowning blow. That guy was a jerkoff.

Too many teams in the league are playing with a Ouija board, playing with bad people. You need good citizens. It appalled me how many bad people there were in the NBA.

People often ask me about the drug problem in the league. Well, personally I didn't see it, but that didn't mean it wasn't around. You've got to understand, I am naive when it comes to hard drugs. I wouldn't even know what cocaine looked like. My naivete was part of my problem. I still thought you stood up for the national anthem.

I was appalled by the high salaries the players commanded, an average contract, at the time, of $107,000 a year. That's a lot of money. What was I supposed to do, babysit these guys? Was I supposed to go on the road and worry which guy was drinking beer or smoking pot or screwing some local broad? God only knows what they were doing in their hotel rooms.

As for the league's future, unless the NBA takes note of its problems and confronts the issues, they are going to be in for a tough time. The ownership is the reason the NBA will die. It's not the players. Same goes for professional baseball. All pro leagues have got to find solutions for free agency, the astronomical salaries, the large egos and the overall lack of discipline displayed by ownership.

For instance, an NBA owner will not remove a player from his team if he finds out the guy is on drugs. Sometimes they look the other way. Technically, a general manager is supposed to report drug violations by players to the owner, who in turn is responsible for calling the NBA commissioner. But it doesn't happen. The owner doesn't want reports circulating that it is his organization which has drug problems. Nobody wants to step forward and help. Everyone keeps quiet and hides in his personal closet. It's very sad.

14
IN SEARCH OF
TOMORROW

There is nothing like being holed up in Buffalo in the middle of January. Especially with about 30 inches of snow outside and no place to go. I was unemployed...and I had no place to go.

I had been relieved of my duties with the Braves on the 25th of January and about three days later the great blizzard of '77 hit and paralyzed the city. So I was stuck there. Finally, we got a warm spell and some of the snow melted. I split, leaving Nancy and the kids behind. I had to get away by myself.

I stopped at a bunch of places, first at Ohio Wesleyan to see my old alma mater play. Then I went on to Miami (Ohio) and Louisville, watched a couple of ballgames, and took off for South Carolina to visit my folks in Easley, a small town about 15 miles outside of Clemson. From there I went to Wrightsville Beach in North Carolina and stayed with a friend at his condominium for a month. I did a lot of thinking and very little eating. My weight dropped from 195 pounds to 170. I didn't eat anything but vegetables and fish, ran every day about eight miles, and grew another beard. I just wanted to escape from society.

I hardly saw or talked with anyone.

After this month, the cloud began to lift and I interviewed for several jobs. Some were in business, like a manufacturer's representative. I talked to a lot of people on the phone, trying to find something I could do, some job which I would enjoy. Finally, at the end of February, I went to the ACC tournament. I just wanted to see if I could return to an old environment and handle it. I did.

It was a slow process, but I was gradually shedding the ill feelings which I had kept deep inside, feelings left over from Clemson and from Buffalo. I analyzed what had happened, where I had failed in my coaching career. For the first time in almost three years I felt good about myself. Furthermore, I concluded I didn't fail with the Braves because of my coaching ability, but rather because I was too inexperienced for a head position in the NBA. It simply was a bad move, one which I had made in haste.

I thought about the immorality of my sins at Clemson, which initially got me to thinking about writing a book on my experiences. Before I could take pen in hand, however, I knew I had to get over my hatred for what had transpired at Clemson. If I had written a book at this stage in my life, surely it would have been very vindictive, not a message which was going to reach out to others in the coaching profession and educate them about life in the fast lane. I wanted to let my colleagues know, particularly the younger ones starting out, of the personal hell they are letting themselves in for if they subscribe to under-the-table recruiting methods. If you have a conscience at all, it will only destroy you as a human being. Believe me, I know.

I was on the brink of doing something rash with my life in the winter of 1977, but I guess the thing which saved me was knowing I didn't have a chance to succeed in Buffalo. In other words, I didn't leave Buffalo believing I had failed, waiting for the end of the world. After my dismissal at Clemson, I had felt like I was going to die. Why I didn't commit suicide or have a nervous breakdown I'll never really know. I really thought I was going to die after Clemson. After Buffalo, all I was doing was feeling sorry for myself.

I was determined to carry on with my life...with one stipulation: that I would spend the next year completely away from basketball. Frankly, it was an ideal time to attempt such a withdrawal since the Braves had another year and a half to pay me off on my two-year, $40,000 per season contract. Legally, they had the obligation, though eventually I'd have to accept a $25,000 settlement.

But I had some money coming in, so I decided to pack up the family and move back to Easley, to be close with my parents. Nancy wasn't fond of the idea—she never did take to Easley—but she agreed to go. Next assignment was to find a job. I wound up going to work for Pete Martin as a manufacturer's representative, the same line of work as my father. It didn't take me long, however, to realize I wasn't cut out to do that line of work. Pete knew it, too. He knew I wasn't going to stay in the business for long, but he was nice enough to let me hang my hat in town for a year.

Going door-to-door, selling things, bothered me, probably because I had to answer so many of the same questions about Clemson. I was back in the same area with many of the same individuals who had done me in two years before, facing them eyeball to eyeball. In some respects I enjoyed it. I guess you might say I was spiteful. I wanted to go back in there and live in their bellies. It was something I had to do for my own piece of mind. I wanted to see some of those folks squirm, especially those who had made my parents feel uncomfortable.

My parents and I never discussed it much, but I'm sure mom and dad took some abuse. I'm sure they were embarrassed.

"Oh, people weren't really that bad, they didn't say a whole lot to my face," remembered Ed Locke, now 72 and retired. "But then you have to remember the people we talked to the most were our friends and they weren't the type to throw dirt in your face. If anyone did bring up the issue, usually I'd say, 'Well, he got caught with his hand in the cookie jar but I'm sure somebody else's hand was in there with him.' I told people that I didn't know who was at fault.

"Actually his biggest fault at Clemson was Tates wanting to do things to please a whole lot of people. By God, you can't please everyone all the time. Unfortunately, some of the fellas who got him started on the wrong track were the same people he tried to please the most...and some of them were the same ones who got out of the way (during the NCAA investigation) and let him fall.

"I really had no knowledge of what was going on at the time because Tates never confided in me and I never pressed the issue. Oh, sometimes I think I asked him who had blown the whistle on him and he'd say 'quite a few did' but Tates would never get specific.

"I know some people have said my son could 'con anybody around', that this bad habit was a direct result of him being spoiled as an only child. I only agree with part of that. Yes, Tates does have a great way with words—he can pretty much lead people the way he wants them to be lead. But spoiled? I don't think so. There was never a time, as a youngster, that he wasn't out working. Not because we told him he had to work, but because he enjoyed working with his hands. He'd put up fences, paint...do almost anything.

"Tates was a good boy as a child, getting into no more trouble than the average boy. He always seemed to have a keen interest in helping other kids, especially the younger ones. For instance, when we were in Cincinnati and Tates was a senior at Indian Hill High School, he'd get up at six in the morning to bring seventh and eighth grade kids over to the gym to teach them basketball. It's almost as if he were born to teach the sport.

"Of course, I had other plans for him. Not that I didn't enjoy and follow his athletic activities, but being the only child I had kind of hoped Tates would come into business with me. He was an extroverted person, the kind which lends itself to my business, but his interest in sports gravitated him toward that profession.

"It never really bothered me a whole lot that he chose sports and coaching. I'd rather see him do something he enjoyed. There's no sense putting a square plug into a round hole.''

Dad was right I wasn't cut out to be a salesman. By Christmas of 1977 I was bored with my job and ready to give coaching another try. But was basketball ready for me again? That was the key question.

I had to find out.

That fall I had slowly drifted back to the local high school and college gyms to watch teams practice but it wasn't until spending a miserable Christmas that I realized I needed to do more than watch. My life was absurd. There I was in Easley masquerading as a salesman when I was one of the best damn coaches in the business. I thought to myself, 'Hey, coaching is your life. You gotta get back in.'

I plotted a return, carefully stacking the cards in my favor. First, I called Bobby Knight—who else?—and told him about my desire. Bobby's only question was, 'Are you sure?' I convinced him I was, so Bobby went to bat for me. Next I contacted Frank McGuire at South Carolina, Dave Bliss at Oklahoma, N. C. State's Norm Sloan and Joe Williams of Florida State. I called a couple of administrators, Paul Dietzel, the athletic director at South Carolina, and Ralph Floyd, an assistant AD at Indiana.

I even contacted the NCAA in Kansas City and someone in the front office told me they would help to get me a coaching job...or at least speak in my behalf if a school inquired.

I was trying to be up front with everyone, so much so that I would volunteer information about my situation at Clemson when I was interviewed for several jobs. I would tell them, ''I think it's in your best interest to call the NCAA and let them explain the situation.''

What amazed me was how few knew about my past involvement at Clemson.

A couple of months passed and I was still unemployed. I was beginning to lose confidence in myself. I also got a little paranoid, though I never thought I was being blackballed out of college coaching by the NCAA as some of my friends suggested. But I did have a feeling that everybody hated Tates Locke.

Actually, the people at the NCAA couldn't have been any nicer. The same for Dr. Edwards at Clemson. I had called Edwards that winter to ask if the school would give a solid recommendation and he promised me it would. It's funny what motivates people to be nice at that point. Were they ashamed of what happened? Were they ashamed of what they had done to me professionally? I don't know, I really don't. But all this sudden cooperation caught me offguard. Even Dean Smith offered to help.

Eventually I was offered head coaching positions at five schools, including Northern Arizona, California at Santa Barbara, Furman and Jacksonville. There were not a helluva lot of UCLA's knocking at my door.

When I saw the situation at Jacksonville, a school with an outlaw image in need of a fresh coat of paint, I knew the job was for me.

I was hired in March, the week before the NCAA tournament. In many respects I was amazed at the similarities between JU and Clemson. For instance my predecessor, Don Beasley, had depended on others to get him players. The school had an assistant coach, Andy Russo, who in his desire to get blue chip players overlooked the NCAA rulebook. There was even a bagman—an alumnus with big bucks—who was behind much of the wheeling and dealing.

Beasley was basically a good person and a decent coach. He just lost control, as I had done at Clemson. I recall reading a newsclip from a story in the Florida *Times Union* in which Beasley said, "I believe a great deal in my players. Good coaches have good players, poor coaches have poor players. I don't say that in a negative way, but if you get good players that's the first requisite to being successful...talented players don't absolutely insure that you will win, however. Once you acquire some you have to get them to play together as a team."

Poor Don never could accomplish that on or off the court. His first squad went 13-13 but in 1976-77 the Dolphins fell off to a 10-19 record. Even a .500 season (14-14) in 1977-78 couldn't save him. By then, the team was uncontrollable. I remember Phil Parisi, a guard who played three seasons for me at JU, telling the story of how players cursed Beasley on the bench, right to his face. They stabbed him in his back.

Parisi told me: "Some of the players were even drinking booze during the games. They'd bring some rum and add it to the cokes. They'd hide the rum in their uniform jacket, then dump it into the cokes when the coach wasn't looking. It made me wonder what else they were doing in the dorms."

When I first held discussions with JU administrators about some of the problems, I couldn't help think about the irony of the situation. Here I was walking into a situation which someone else had created, very similar to the kind of situation I had left for my successor, Bill Foster, at Clemson.

I told the administration that I thought the school could get good basketball players *without* cheating. I told them that in my first interview, which lasted over two hours. The school asked me what I knew about Jacksonville University and I mentioned I had discussed the school's history with former JU coach, Joe Williams, a fellow who directed them to a 27-2 season and within one victory of the NCAA title in 1969-70, his final season at JU before moving to Furman. The reputation of the school, from what I had been told, was that the city, the community and the JU boosters wanted a basketball program more than the school itself.

Basically, this was going to be JU's final shot at big-time basketball. If the Dolphins couldn't make it, the school was considering dropping its Division I status to Division II.

I liked that kind of a challenge and figured it would be a great opportunity. Here was a school with its back to the wall and here I was, a coach, with my back to the wall. Each of us were going to get one final shot at the big time. With that as a foundation, I saw it as a pretty good marriage for both sides.

I told JU what I stood for—the American flag, national anthem and Converse shoes. All that kind of good stuff. And I told them I was going to bring that to be at Jacksonville if given the opportunity. We would start slowly and go on from there.

Looking back, maybe I was daydreaming. Maybe it'll never happen at Jacksonville, but I like to think it could have.

15
GUNS . . . BUT NO BASKETBALLS

I wasn't in my office for more than a week when two Jacksonville players paid me a visit. Jimmy Martin and Phil Parisi were guards on Don Beasley's 1977-78 team, two decent kids who it appeared had been banged around by all the turmoil at school. I sensed they were rather lonely, probably because they were outcasts among their teammates.

The two of them talked up a storm during our first meeting. It was obvious they wanted to get some things off their chests and let me know where they were coming from. So I listened. Some of the stories were unbelievable, tales so horrible it made Clemson seem like a peaceful place. For instance, Phil told me there were no basketballs left in the gymnasium equipment room. He said it had been raided by the team and cleaned out. I found it hard to believe, so I took a look for myself. Parisi was right.

Not only weren't there any basketballs, but all the uniforms were missing. All the sneakers, too, except for two...and they didn't match. Only a few bars of soap remained, along with several rolls of adhesive tape and a can of foot powder. That was the extent of my basketball equipment.

Finding players wasn't easy, either. From several discussions I had with Beasley and his assistant, Andy Russo, I learned there was talent in the program. There were some bona fide players, like 6-8 forward Ron Anthony, a high school All-American, 6-5 forward Dwayne Smith, 6-9 center James Ray and Anthony "Cricket" Williams, a solid guard.

There also was a 6-7 junior forward out of Louisville named Flenoil Crook, a rather unlikely but appropriate name for this prep All-American and first team junior college (Pensacola JC) All-American. Flenoil had averaged 10 points a game in 1977-78, fourth best on the squad behind Anthony (19.4), Smith (14.8) and Ray (12.8). Crook had great timing, was a good passer and excellent rebounder. He was the kind of ballplayer who could swing between forward and guard.

Flenoil, I had been told, wasn't a bad shot with a basketball...or with a gun. Yeah, a gun.

Around the time of my arrival, Flenoil had gotten himself into hot water with the local authorities for shooting teammate Donnie Tyler, a troublemaking senior who I had been told was the ringleader behind many of JU's past problems, including several knife-stabbing incidents. Anyway, Parisi told me Tyler had stabbed Crook on a previous occasion and this was Flenoil's way of retaliating. Phil also told me Crook was likely to be looking for him and Jimmy Martin because the two of them had argued with Crook shortly before he shot Tyler. Crook, they suspected, would come after them next.

I remember the day the police were on campus, conducting a dorm-to-dorm search for Crook. Martin and Parisi stayed in their room the whole time and locked the door. They were scared shitless. So was I, particularly after the police asked me to go into Flenoil's dorm room and bring him out. The cops told me, "Hey, he's your player."

I was on campus for less than a month and never met the kid and he's *my* player. Hmmm.

Over the years, there have been more than a quota of amusing stories attached to the Jacksonville U. basketball program. Of course, many go back to the days when Artis Gilmore played for Joe Williams in 1970-71, when a lot of hands were supposedly stuffed with cash from the alumni. There was a story of how 2,000 tickets suddenly got "lost" one season, right under the eyes of the athletic department.

Another time, I believe it was in 1974, Henry Williams and Shawn Leftwich showed their IQ by attempting to cash checks given illegally to them by agents trying to negotiate professional contracts. Leftwich and Williams took the checks over to the JU administration building and tried to cash them. I mean, how stupid can you be? Not surprisingly, they both lost their college eligibility.

Another story took place during my first season. We had a freshman recruit from South Carolina who was this country's first scholarship basketball player from India. Singh Guram, a 6-7, slightly built forward, was a very likeable kid, but he was sometimes gullible. Dwayne Smith once tried to fence a stolen icebox to Singh, who was eager to make the transaction. Parisi was around at the time and was amazed at the price—he thought Smith wasn't getting enough for the icebox. It wasn't until Jimmy Martin arrived and told Guram and Parisi the box was "hot" that the kids came to their senses.

Imagine the task of molding this outfit into a respectable team by the start of the 1978-79 season?

My first official move in the spring was to buy six basketballs, at $30 each, so the players had an excuse to practice when the mood hit them. I also purchased some tee-shirts with "JU Basketball" on the front. I figured now there was no excuse for not knowing who they were. I also worked on having the school get us a training room...a few simple pleasures like a whirlpool, rubbing table, etc. I couldn't believe they didn't already have one.

Like I said, JU was a sorry sight when I got there.

Finally, I made time to recruit. We went out and got Mike Hackett, a well-muscled, 6-5 forward from Orangeburg, South Carolina, and 6-3 guard Paul DeVito of De Matha High School in Hyattsville, Maryland. My assistant coach, Tom Barrise, helped recruit a youngster from his hometown, 6-9 center Barlow Taylor of Paterson, New Jersey. We rounded out our hunt with forward Pete Boyle of Centerville, Ohio, and Stan Conley, a guard from Brandon, Florida.

By the time we started fall practice, Ron Anthony had been dismissed from school and Flenoil Crook was in jail. Two of our top four scorers were gone and the only senior was Crickett Williams, who gave us leadership in the backcourt. Underneath we got leadership from James Ray, plus some critical points and rebounds. James was a youngster out of New Orleans who proved to be the offensive backbone of our club over the next two seasons. Without him we could have gone down the tubes.

In that first season, we split our initial eight contests, including a two-point opening loss to Wake Forest and a 29-point drubbing at the hands of North Carolina. In those early games, Hackett, not Ray, proved to be our most dependable player.

Shortly after Christmas our fortunes changed, beginning with a home court win over Georgia State on December 19. That improved our record to 5-4 and started us on a seven-game winning streak, including wins against Pittsburgh, Florida and Florida State. Now we were 11-4 and it seemed my patience was paying handsome dividends.

I had laid everything on the line with my players from the start, both personally and professionally. I told them everything they wanted to know about my past...every little detail. In fact, I said if at any time they wanted to examine transcripts from the NCAA investigation at Clemson they were welcome to visit my office and the read the literature. I was very insistent upon them understanding my position—that there would be no rulebending or money passed around as long as I was at Jacksonville. My cheating days were history. I had no choice; too many eyes would be watching me and if I got caught again my career would be finished. I knew this, the administration knew it and I wanted my players to know it.

Until I heard Parisi mention it later, I was not aware JU players mixed rum and coke during ballgames when Beasley was coach, but I was aware there had been a general laxity of the rules. I knew about the misuse of rental cars, how certain players would take them out for rides the night after a road game, then return them the next day in Jacksonville. I told the players I would not stand for that.

"I don't think coach Beasley was naive," Parisi told me when I questioned him, "but I don't think he realized the players were capable of doing so much. He didn't think that they were *that* crazy. Coach tried to be a disciplinarian but he had no control. He never made an example of anybody.

"I remember the time we played at Western Kentucky and Flenoil made a costly turnover along the baseline. Coach said something to Flenoil and he turned around and told coach to 'suck my - - - -' I looked over at Jimmy Martin and we couldn't believe it.

"Coach took Flenoil out but then put him right back in. Ironically, Crook made the shot which sent the game into overtime."

I was determined to avoid those kinds of problems. When we got off to that fast start, I was led to believe there would be no such trouble.

South Florida came along and snapped the winning streak January 15 at our Coliseum, but we recovered to beat North Carolina-Charlotte in overtime and the University of New Orleans by one point. Next stop was Mobile, Alabama and we lost to South Alabama by nine points. That was on a Monday. Saturday we came back to beat Alabama-Birmingham, lifting our overall record to 14-6

We traveled to Charlotte on January 30 and it was while we were on this trip that Pete Boyle came forth and told me about our squad's drug problem. The news hit me like a bomb.

The witch hunt began after we lost to NC-Charlotte by five points. The next morning, before we flew home, I called in every member of the team, individually, and gave them the opportunity to confess. By then, thanks to Boyle, I knew who the guilty ones were. It took a lot of guts on Pete's part to come forth because this incident eventually ended his collegiate basketball career. From that moment on, the guilty players made it tough on him.

I was anxious to see which players would own up to doing drugs and smoking pot. After questioning everyone, I suspended Hackett and Smith. Both had lied to me, probably afraid of what I might do. The players who admitted their involvement—Ray, Boyle, Greg Harris and Frankie Lemmons—were all put on probation for the remainder of the season. They were allowed to play because they told me the truth.

Hackett and Smith were dismissed, but I promised I would reinstate them for the 1979-80 season if they got their acts together. Hackett worked like a trojan the rest of the season and eventually returned; Smith continued to cut corners and never played again at JU. He later transferred to Eastern Kentucky.

Without Smith and Hackett, our second and third leading scorers and two of our top rebounders, we lost three of the next four games, dropping to 15-9. We were floundering and I know some people questioned my decision to drop Smith and Hackett. There was a feeling that perhaps I had overreacted. Hell, no way. I decided, win or lose, no player was going to ignore team rules. My rules! If they broke them they would have to suffer the consequences. I was not going to fall into the same trap as Beasley. Not over my dead body.

Fortunately, the team rallied behind James Ray. I guess they wanted to prove something and they did. I was very proud of that team. We concluded the regular season by knocking off South Carolina, 79-68, then pulled off a stunning sweep of the Sun Belt Conference tournament in Charlotte. In succession we defeated New Orleans, South Alabama and South Florida. That earned us a spot in the NCAA tournament field, the school's first appearance since 1973.

We met Virginia Tech in the opening round of the Mid-West Regionals and lost, 70-53. Had we won we would have faced Indiana State, which had a pretty fair player by the name of Larry Bird. That would have been interesting, but what the heck, we finished in a blaze of glory. Considering our mid-season problems, 19-9 wasn't bad for openers.

After the Tech game I walked the streets for hours, reflecting back on my first season. I was very happy, but at the same time disappointed. I began looking forward to bigger and better seasons. Maybe I was getting delusions of grandeur, but that is only natural with most of us basketball coaches. Coaches are pigs—they're never satisfied, not even those fellows who go 32-0 as Bobby Knight did in 1976. There is always a feeling of accomplishing more.

Unfortunately, we took a step backward at JU.

Except for Crickett Williams, we had everyone returning for the 1979-80 season, including Hackett. All we needed was a decent recruiting session but we didn't land anyone. The four prospects we eventually signed—Linwood Davis, Dolan Douglas, Maurice Roulhac and Bobby Stovall—were not much help. Only Roulhac, with a 6.6 scoring average, contributed. Stovall had a 1.7 mark and Douglas and Davis made just one basket each.

Going into the season, I knew everything would fall on James Ray's shoulders. I said a prayer every night that he wouldn't get hurt.

Amazingly, we started off 10-0, thanks mostly to the experience and confidence gained on our summer trip to China. We went undefeated over there and came back home with great momentum. We thought no team could beat us, and, in reality, it wasn't until the sixth week of the season when NC-Charlotte and South Alabama handed us back-to-back losses.

But again we rallied to win six straight for a 16-2 mark and a spot in the Top 20 nationally.

Then we slumped. We lost three straight, five out of seven and seven of our last 11 games. We finished 20-9, losing to Murray State in the first round of the NIT. Down the stretch, we lacked a team leader, a role Paul DeVito would have played had he not dropped out of school prior to the season. We missed Paul badly.

Now my staff and I went back to the drawing board. Because we had made it to the NCAAs and NIT in successive seasons was no cause to relax. This time around we had to get a big man and a couple of strong guards. James Ray was graduating and someone had to take his place. If nothing else, we needed a center.

Again we came up short. The three freshman we brought in, forwards Terry Bush and Andy Williams and guard Garry Grier, were not the answer.

Our first mistake was not finding a replacement for James Ray. The second mistake was letting myself get soft. Quite honestly, I let too many players get away with bad habits in 1980-81.

When you go 8-19 it isn't entirely the fault of the players. Oh, I remember telling a Richmond reporter that "this team may be my worst team ever, worse than the one I had in '70-71 at Clemson" and in truth it might have been my worst club. But I didn't help them very much. Maybe with a lot of veterans returning I assumed the players knew my philosophies. I, in turn, trusted their maturity.

Many of the players took advantage of my new posture, especially when it came to being punctual for practice. All throughout the season players drifted in late for practice, offering weak excuses. I accepted it. In the past, I would have punished them for the first offense and kicked them off the team if it happened again. Now I was giving them third, fourth and fifth chances.

The players were also a little overconfident in their abilities. I don't know why—there wasn't a helluva lot of talent. I guess they figured JU had won 19 and 20 games the previous seasons so they could turn it on whenever they wanted.

If you asked the players, I think they would agree. I got soft.

"Coach was right," Phil Parisi admitted. "He didn't have the same intensity as he did in the first two seasons. I remember his first season, after we lost to North Park at home. Was he upset. He walked toward the locker room and kicked the door right off its hinges. The door wouldn't open so he kicked it in.

"You always had it in the back of your mind that he could get violent. Don't get me wrong—I don't think he'd grab players like Knight—but he always kept you wondering. Once he told us he had thrown a soda can at a player, so every time he had a soda in his hand you would wonder if he was gonna throw it at you. I was always ready to duck.''

We began the 1980-81 season very slowly, losing four of our first five games. We didn't even score 50 points in three of the defeats, losing 45-40 in the Palestra against St. Joseph's. Forty points in 40 minutes!

So I got a little tougher with the kids and they responded. We split six games, then beat NC-Charlotte and Georgia State, the doormat of the Sun Belt Conference. Now we stood at 6-7 with an opportunity to reach .500 at home against St. Joe's.

We lost by two...this time we scored 42 points. Poor execution, no poise. We had lost all confidence in our abilities.

If there was a turning point to our season, it was the loss to St. Joe's. From there on we played to lose close, dropping 10 of 11. Our only victory came at NC-Charlotte but before we could enjoy that one we came back and lost to Georgia State. Rotten Georgia State. That was the clincher.

"He was like a madman after that game," Parisi recalled. "You could see the frustration in his eyes. He came into the locker room and turned red. Then he began punching lockers. He called us a bunch of losers and challenged anyone to stand up and deny it. He was ready to fight somebody. He punched one locker so hard I swore he broke his hand.

"I know there were a couple of guys who wanted to fight him that night, not because they disliked Coach, but because of what he was saying to their faces. He can get a guy mad. When he called us a bunch of chokes I thought someone was going to pop him. I think he's lucky no one did. He might have met his match that night. We were mad.

"Tates never was the easiest guy to play for, especially if you were a guard. During games, Coach always had what he called 'designated goats.' What that meant was if he got upset with a ref's call, he'd scream at the ref but look right at the player who was designated his goat. He'd be kicking the press table or ripping off his coat and looking at you all the time. Anybody could be the designated goat but it usually was a guard, either me or Jimmy (Martin).''

Contrary to what some members of the JU administration believed, I don't think I ever worked harder with a team than I did with the '80-81 squad in January and February. If we could have won the St. Joe's game and reached .500 it might have been an entirely different season. One game can make that much of a difference.

You have to have confidence to play this game and by the third week of January we didn't have an ounce of confidence. We were waiting for bad breaks to happen, which sort of reminded me of those final months with the Buffalo Braves.

When we got into the thick of our slump, some of the kids even started to question my coaching philosophies. It's bound to happen when you lose. People naturally like to point fingers at someone else. And it seemed all eyes—and fingers—were pointing at me.

I decided there was only one way out of this mess—go out and have a super recruiting season. That meant spending a lot of my time away from the team. By February the season was lost; I knew my club wasn't going anywhere, so I let my assistants run some of the practices and I took off on the road to recruit. We had done poorly the past two seasons using mainly assistant coaches and I felt this time around I needed to be in the home of every prospect. I needed to be at the kid's school, to meet his coach and watch him practice. And I did that.

We had some outstanding prospects coming to JU. Calvin Duncan, a 6-4 guard from Oak Hill Academy in Virginia, was our No. 1 recruit and looked to be the most talented player at JU since James Ray. We also were right in the hunt with North Carolina for 7-1 Warren Martin, another prospect from Virginia. Our No. 3 recruit was Al Butts out of Philadelphia, who along with Steve Black, also of Philly, played for Frederick Military Academy in Virginia. Another good prospect was 6-10 Dave Reickenicker, a Floridian who wound up with Tommy Barrise at East Carolina University. We had some good prospects, kids who I felt could win 15 or 16 games in 1981-82.

Now, I guess we'll never know, will we?

Coach Jack Ramsey and his assistant coach, Tates Locke in March, 1976. (Above)

Head Buffalo coach Tates Locke makes a point in the huddle as assistant coach Charlie Harrison, right, looks on. (Left)

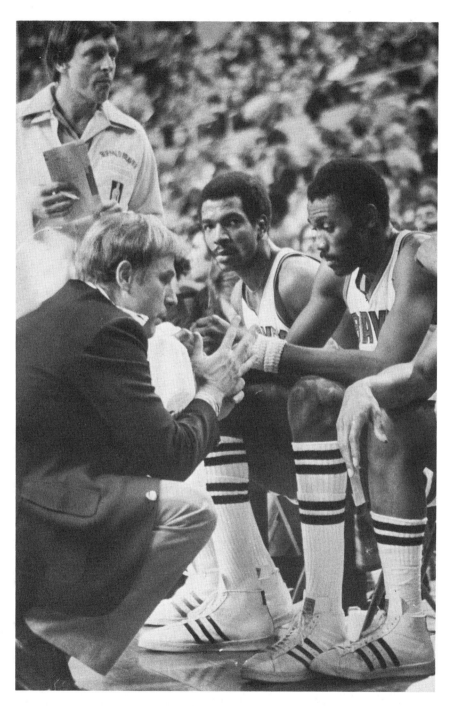

Head coach Tates Locke of The Buffalo Braves talks to Bob McAdoo,
right, and Randy Smith, left, on the bench during a time out in a
December 7, (1976) game, one month before Locke was fired.

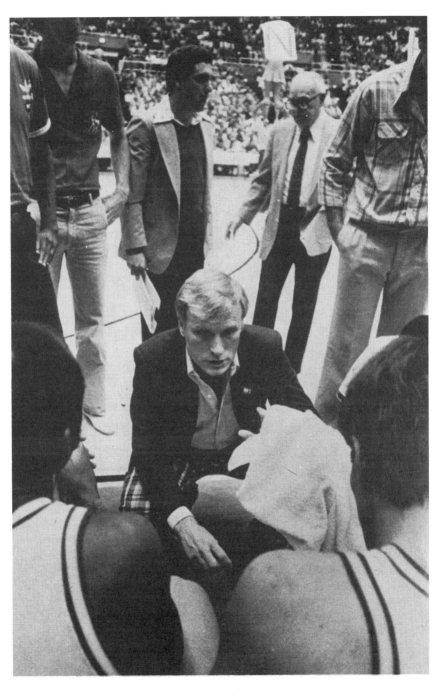

Head coach Tates Locke discusses strategy with his Jacksonville team during a time out (March, 1980).

Dr. Frances Kinne, President of Jacksonville University.

Flenoil Crook, ex-Jacksonville player.

Ed Locke, Tates's father, sits next to his son.

The Locke family (Nancy, Kathy, Mike, Tates, and John) in happier days at Clemson.

Nancy Locke (November, 1981).

John, Mike, and Kathy Locke—Tates' children.

Duty, honor, country.

EPILOGUE

16
LOOKING FOR ANSWERS

It hasn't been an easy decision to pour out my innermost thoughts and feelings on the subject of the illegal recruitment of college athletes, specifically using my own experiences at Clemson University as a point of focus. I realize many of my critics won't believe me when I say I have done a lot of soul-searching, going back to probably that last season at Clemson in '75, before deciding to undertake this project.

Caught in the Net has been in the back of my mind almost continuously since my departure from Clemson. The thought of writing the book occurred to me again while I was coaching in Buffalo, and still later at Jacksonville University. I guess I didn't get *serious* about the book, however, until discussing the details with co-author Bob Ibach on a visit to Philadelphia in early December of 1980, just before we played St. Joseph's. Before that discussion, I had briefed my wife and a few close friends about the idea of a book. Nancy finally came around to agreeing with me that the book should be written, but there were several friends who tried to get me to change my mind. They thought it would serve no purpose, and, even if it did, might ruin me professionally. They told me the risks were far too great.

I'd be lying if I didn't admit to wavering just a little myself over the winter months of 1981, wondering if my intentions would be misunderstood by the media and the public. I wanted people to understand that I wasn't writing a book to "get back at certain people" as some thought, but actually in the hope some other young college coach might read about my self-inflicted downfall and avoid a similar embarrassment.

I still feel that way. If this book does nothing else but help just *one* coach out there who is going through the same hell I went through, then it will have served its purpose.

I guess what solidified my belief in this project occurred two months before my dismissal at Jacksonville. We were playing an afternoon game in Mobile, Alabama against South Alabama. Jim Thacker, a popular television sports commentator who broadcasts Sun Belt Conference games, approached me about accompanying him to Clemson after our contest. Thacker was scheduled to do the play-by-play of the South Carolina-Clemson game and thought I might be interested in coming along on their private airplane. I agreed to make the trip.

Arriving at Littlejohn Coliseum that evening brought back a lot of memories. For me, the nostalgia was heavy. I mean, you don't spend five years of your life in a small town like Clemson and walk away entirely. A piece of me always remained there.

Sitting at one of the press tables at courtside, my eyes wandered through the crowd. The faces were familiar, sometimes *too* familiar. I guess that is what aroused my emotions. I couldn't get over how certain members of the Clemson alumni and athletic department were sitting in exactly the same seats they had occupied when I had been head coach. They were all carrying on the same way. It was like one big party all over again, giving me the feeling I had slipped into some kind of a time machine. It was 1975 all over again, even though I knew the calendar read 1981.

It happened these same people were doing the same illegal things as before...that obviously, no one had learned a lesson. No one had walked away from the dirt of the early 1970s. They just *never* walked away. I saw that and I got this sick feeling in my stomach.

From that moment on, I knew *Caught in the Net* had to be completed.

****

First off, let me say this: I think it is difficult to say which schools and coaches are *not* cheating. I am sure there are some who are not, but you start discussing the illegal recruitment of a college athlete and you are talking about the *degree* of cheating, not the actual act of cheating itself.

What induces a certain ballplayer to attend a particular college? Let's start there. Every high school player in this country, when he begins talking about playing Division I basketball, has to have a reason for attending the school he selected. Some will tell you it is because of the academic environment but actually what has transpired is that the institution, more than likely the coach, has told this youngster "we can get you through school if you are a poor student."

That, friends, is an inducement.

You are promising this kid something you have no right to promise him—guaranteed passing grades.

If this appears to be innocent, perhaps it is, but such an inducement is only the beginning. Once a school skirts the academic part, the next step is to assist the youngster with his campus lifestyle. They may offer him transportation to and from his home, or maybe an alumnus will offer a special deal on clothing. Or it could be a discount on an automobile. It just mushrooms. And, for those universities which are doing it big-time, the favors go beyond this stage. There are offers and promises made to a recruit's parents. Sometimes the school may build them a new home or buy them furniture. Or simply pay them off in cash.

I'm always amused when I attend NCAA conventions and tournaments and see the parents of these youngsters. You look at them and their economic background and know there is no way possible they paid their own way. And I know their community didn't hold a local street dance to raise the money. Yet time after time I see these parents after ballgames coming to campus from 200 to 1,000 miles away.

How the hell do you think they're getting to campus?

I know Charlie Harrison used to tell me one of the first things he looked for when he was recruiting was whether or not the recruit automatically expected you to offer him something. Charlie told me—and he was right—a kid doesn't jump to that conclusion unless another school had been into his home before and offered him something illegal. That is a tipoff right there.

The inducements are made smoothly. Colon Abraham once told me he never saw the money B.C. Inabinet was sending him for his new car, but he knew his parents received the money on a regular basis at the end of each month through the mail. Colon never felt guilty about taking the money because he had given Clemson a lot of his time and ability and helped the school earn even more money from ticket receipts.

I believe there is a message for other college basketball coaches somewhere in my final season at Jacksonville University, in our miserable 8-19 record. As Al McGuire used to say, "with one aircraft carrier you could have flipped-flopped that record around."

Al was right. During the 1980-81 season our team averaged 57.5 points a game. Our opponents averaged 59 points. So we lost, on the average, by 1.5 points, which shows you what one "aircraft carrier" would have meant to us. The guy could have been 6-5 or 7-0 or 5-10, but one outstanding athlete could have turned our season around without question.

The problem begins when you consider the importance of getting this "aircraft carrier." You look at the prospect and say to yourself, 'Boy, we *need* that guy.' Then it starts. After you get the one kid, you want two. Then you get the second prospect and you want another...and another. It snowballs. By then you've lost control.

I never lost control at Jacksonville as I had at Clemson. Eventually my honesty caught up with me. By going 8-19 in 1980-81, by having two horren-

dous recruiting seasons back-to-back at Jacksonville, proved to me everything I have felt about recruiting since I was dismissed from Clemson.
Beliefs which I felt and the hatred I had for the system since 1975 were prov-
en true—if you recruit honestly most likely you'll end up with a losing team.

Recruiting done strictly according to the NCAA rulebook is almost an
impossibility, but schools and coaches *can* skim the top of legalities and cut
down on the flagrant violations. That is a very realistic goal.

For instance, if I were coaching at Indiana or Ohio State, I don't think
I'd have to flagrantly cheat because you live off your own state kid. You
have loyalties in those states and if a coach is smart enough to wrap his tentacles around the football people he can survive and do quite well in his
basketball program. Why anybody at schools like those would have to cheat
I'll never know.

What about the private institutions? Well, I don't know enough about
the workings at a Notre Dame to comment, but I can tell you about the
setup at a military school like Army. When I was at West Point, we were not
allowed to pay for a young man's visit to the Academy. So are you going to
tell me we got Mike Silliman, a two-time first team high school All-American, without paying his way to West Point for a visit? Come on.

We did pay his way but that wasn't in violation of any NCAA rule, only a
rule set forth by the Academy.

When Mike Silliman decided to attend the Point, here was a perfect example of harrassment on the part of other schools. He was being recruited
by Kentucky, which threatened to get his father dismissed from his job if
Mike didn't play for Adolph Rupp. Mike, you see, was from the Louisville
area and Kentucky felt it would be disloyal of him to go elsewhere. I believe
the only reason we got Mike to come to West Point was no one could criticize him for attending a military school. That would have been disloyal to
the United States!

The governing body of collegiate basketball, the NCAA, is good in
theory. The NCAA projects itself as a non-profit organization put together
by volunteer members and member institutions for the betterment of inter-
scholastic athletics. That looks very good on paper, but when winning
becomes more important, when money comes next—or maybe it's the other
way around—the NCAA rules won't suffice. College basketball has become
a monster. It's big business. Look at the television monies, tournament
monies and other dollars generated from gate receipts. All those things dic-
tate winning—at all costs.

It's really absurd only a handful of schools are put on probation by the
NCAA. The really big boys are always overlooked. Remember all the garbage which went on at some of the West Coast schools like UCLA and USC
recently? What trash. That whole operation should have been sent into the
ocean. It was as if those schools were giving the NCAA the finger, sitting on

an island and flipping them the bird.

John Wooden was a great basketball coach; I don't think anyone will argue with that. But John was also one of the best in the business at playing the "shell game". Which one is the peanut under? John was clever.

I don't know if Wooden really knew about all the violations or if he even wanted to know. I really doubt if he set them up himself. Regardless, that operation at UCLA was strongly rumored to be the most ruthless cheating game ever established in college basketball which has *never* been caught. The monies, the contracts and financial agreements the players at that school were said to have were totally incredible.

There have been worse leagues than the Pac-10. The greatest bandit league of all-time might have been the Missouri Valley when Cincinnati, Bradley and Wichita were nationally ranked almost every season in the late 50s and 60s.

The Atlantic Coast Conference? I believe a lot of schools in the ACC cheated to get respectable. Clemson was a perfect example. I think years ago there was cheating at North Carolina, heavy cheating, but that subsided when the school got to be respectable and nationally ranked. I think there has been cheating at North Carolina State in the past, but again, it was done to enable the school to catch up with the rest of the pack. Once you get into the pack, and have some money to stay there, if you're smart the cheating decreases. All most alumni want is a chance, every now and then, to make a run at the top. They can live with that at most schools.

I think as long as there are young coaches who want to be head coaches and schools which want to get a piece of the pie, you will always see *some* amount of cheating. The NCAA can't hire enough investigators or make enough rules to stop them. Plus, there is always going to be a double standard of who gets caught and who doesn't. If you are one of the established Top 20 schools and you get caught, more than likely your reprimand will be less severe than say an Idaho State or a Jacksonville or a Clemson. Those are the facts of life in college basketball.

If I can offer one bit of advice to a young coach today, be he a high school head coach or a college assistant, it is that the individual must be willing to accept the unwritten code which already exists. Don't try to change it and don't act surprised and gossip about it. Just go out and get the job done. If it's recruiting, then go out and recruit. Play the game by the rules of the street.

It's like in sales or anything else—somewhere down the line you are going to have to give out green stamps. You are going to have to cheat *somewhere* along the line but do it and don't talk about it.

There is nothing which disturbs me more than to hear a coach say his program is lily white and turn around and gossip about another coach's program. When I hear that kind of talk I call them a liar and walk away. People who know me know I shoot right from where it hurts. I will never talk about them behind their back. I will never tell anyone, 'I didn't get the guy because so and so bought him.' I won't do that. But if a coach starts talking that Mickey Mouse, slobby stuff, I say, 'Hey, wait a minute. You're such an actor. You cheat and you're just disappointed because you didn't get the kid.'

Then I walk away. That's the way I am. Nobody will talk that kind of trash around me. I won't let them. Besides, they should know better. I've *been* there before..

Young coaches had better know what they are getting into before they plunge into the college ranks. I always tell a high school coach, 'I'll help you get a job as a college assistant but don't go walking in there with your eyes closed. Don't think it's going to be all X's and O's and all that strategic stuff. It isn't.''

They all tell me they know they have to recruit players. They'll say, ''I think I can recruit.'' I laugh, then I tell them, 'Yeah, you go recruit but remember to bring a pocket full of money along with you.'

You see, every coach out there can coach; every coach out there can teach. They all can talk. But you have to have something to sell. At Jacksonville, I was fortunate that I had the sun, a small campus and individual academic attention to promote to a recruit. That is more than a lot of coaches have to sell. But I probably didn't have enough. Jacksonville didn't have a beautiful campus arena—we used the city's. And we didn't give away clothing, cars, women and other material items. In that sense, we were operating at a disadvantage.

The end result showed what usually happens. Eight and nineteen.

These days, as I assist head coach Jerry Tarkanian at the University of Nevada-Las Vegas, I'm aware that my coaching career is hanging in limbo. It would take a college administrator with a lot of guts to touch me now, but I had to coach *somewhere* this season. I didn't feel I could afford to sit out a year or else I'd be finished.

Sure, I have a lot of misgivings about my past. It still bothers me that I didn't have enough sense to walk away from the shit going on at Clemson that first season in 1970-71. I had a chance but I didn't walk away.

I laugh when coaches tell me, ''I won't get caught. No one will find out.'' That's all very good. *Don't* get caught. But if you do, then what? If you have a conscience and get caught, what then? I had a conscience. That was my problem. Some coaches can cheat day in and day out and it never bothers them. God bless them. But it bothered me. It tore me apart, wrecked my life, both socially and professionally.

I'm 45 years old now and people ask me why I just don't walk away from basketball and start over again in another profession. I can't. Looking back on my career, there have been more good times than bad. My relationships with players and with other members of the profession like Clair Bee, Joe Lapchick, John Egli, Butch van Breda Kolff and John Bennington will forever be remembered and cherished.

Basketball is more fun for me now than it ever has been, more fun because as you get older you experience more. Imagine if I was 45 and didn't know about all I've discovered so far in college coaching?

My wife says the final chapter about Tates Locke has yet to be written. I hope she is right. My great goal is to play for the national championship. Not necessarily win the thing, but *play* for it, with all things being equal.

Al McGuire once said, "Coaches are the last of the cowboys," but there are fewer and fewer cowboys left. Not many have control of everything. In fact, if you did a national survey, I think you would find very few coaches who have kept their houses clean. Take it from someone who cheated...and got caught.

Tates Locke's
Collegiate Coaching Record

ARMY	(1963-64)	19-7
ARMY	(1964-65)	21-8
MIAMI-OHIO	(1966-67)	14-10
MIAMI-OHIO	(1967-68)	11-12
MIAMI-OHIO	(1968-69)	15-12
MIAMI-OHIO	(1969-70)	16-8
CLEMSON	(1970-71)	9-17
CLEMSON	(1971-72)	10-16
CLEMSON	(1972-73)	12-14
CLEMSON	(1973-74)	14-12
CLEMSON	(1974-75)	17-11
JACKSONVILLE	(1978-79)	19-11
JACKSONVILLE	(1979-80)	20-9
JACKSONVILLE	(1980-81)	8-19
14 YEAR TOTAL		205-156

NIT Appearances - (5)

1964, 1965 (Army)
1970 (Miami-Ohio)
1975 (Clemson)
1980 (Jacksonville)

NCAA Appearances - (2)

1969 (Miami-Ohio)
1979 (Jacksonville)

Other Coaching Experience:

Assistant Coach, Ohio Wesleyan, 1959-60
Assistant Coach, Army, 1960-63
Assistant Coach, Buffalo Braves (NBA), 1975-76
Head Coach, Buffalo Braves (NBA), 1976-77
Assistant Coach, Nevada-Las Vegas, 1981-82